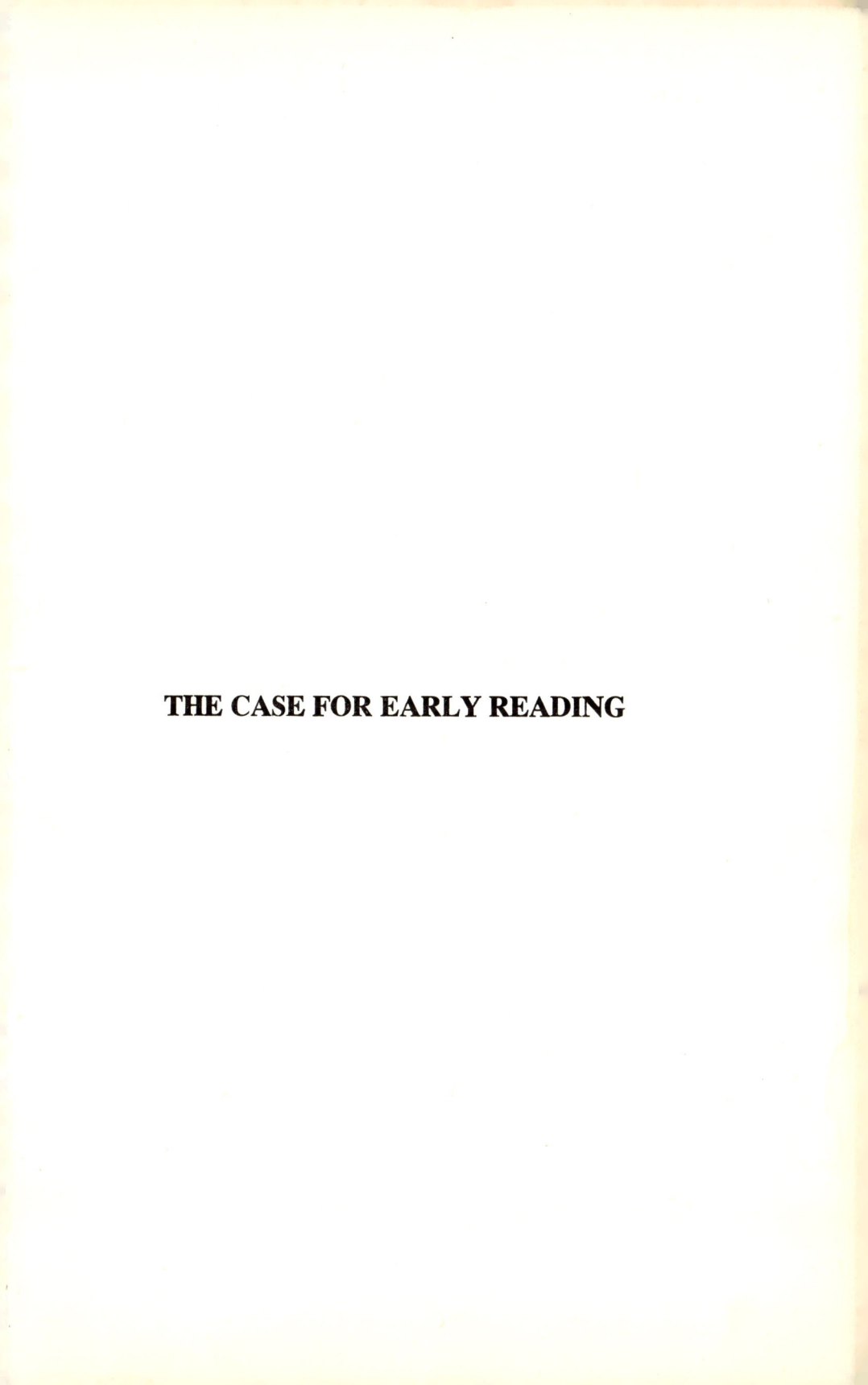

THE CASE FOR EARLY READING

THE CASE FOR EARLY READING

By

GEORGE L. STEVENS, PH.B., M.A.
*Instructor, University College
The University of Maryland*

*Instructor in Reading
Galludet College*

*Reading Consultant
Department of Defense*

Director, Reading Technics

and

R. C. OREM, B.A., M.ED.
*Associate, Planning Research Corporation
Los Angeles and Washington, D.C.*

*Research Adviser
Alcuin Montessori Teacher Training Program*

With a Prologue by
R. BUCKMINSTER FULLER
D. Arts, D. Design, D, Letters, D. Fine Arts,
D. Humane Letters, D. Sc., Etc.

WARREN H. GREEN, INC.
St. Louis, Missouri, U.S.A.

Published by
WARREN H. GREEN, INC.
10 South Brentwood Blvd.
St. Louis, Missouri 63105, U.S.A.

All rights reserved

© 1968 by WARREN H. GREEN, INC.
Library of Congress Catalog Card No. 67-26006

Printed in the United States of America
A-1

LIBRARY
WISCONSIN STATE UNIVERSITY
Stevens Point, Wis. 54481

For
The Students, Staff, and Supporters
of the
World Design Science Decade, 1965-1975
and the
Inventory of World Resources, Human Trends and Needs
Who are designing the comprehensive educational process
For a world literacy product

R. BUCKMINSTER FULLER

Dr. Fuller, the author of the PROLOGUE, has been referred to as ". . . probably the brightest man alive . . ." He is a Professor at Southern Illinois University, is the inventor and designer of the Geodesic Dome, made famous at Expo '67, and has held many important positions and received many honors including: Harvard University Charles Eliot Norton Professor of Poetry; Brandeis University Special Notable Creative Achievement Award for 1964; Delta Phi Delta National Fine Arts Honorary Society, Gold Key Laureate, 1964; Distinguished Scientist Appointment to the U. S. Institute of Behavioral Research, Washington, D. C., and Director of the Center for Study of Human Ecology Transformation, 1965; Vice-President, World Society of Ekistics, 1965; Industrial Designer's Society of America First Award of Excellence, 1966; Graham Foundation Fellow, 1966; First Kassler Memorial Lecturer, Princeton University, 1966; Fellow and Honorary Trustee, Institute of General Semantics. He has received Doctorates in more than a half-dozen fields and has had many other degrees and honors bestowed upon him. Space will not permit a listing of his accomplishments, inventions, honors, teaching positions, lectureships, and special commissions assigned to him by government and industry alike.

PROLOGUE

EMERGENT MAN—HIS ENVIRONMENT AND EDUCATION

By

R. BUCKMINSTER FULLER

Dr. Arts; Dr. Design; Dr. Letters; Dr. F. Arts;
Dr. Humane Letters; Dr. Sc., etc.

An educational revolution is upon us.

One of the most important events of this peaceful but profound revolution is our dawning discovery that the child is born comprehensively competent and co-ordinate, capable of treating with large quantities of data and families of variables right from the start.

Every well-born child is originally geniused, but is swiftly degeniused by unwitting humans and/or physically unfavorable environmental factors. "Bright" children are those less traumatized. Of course, some children have special inbred aptitudes and others, more crossbred, are more comprehensively coordinated.

But the new life is inherently comprehensive in its apprehending, comprehending and coordinating capabilities. The child is interested in the universe. He asks universal questions.

This propensity of the child toward comprehensivity, given a properly patterned environment, is attested in such works as Benjamin Bloom's *Stability and Change in Human Characteristics*,[1] and Wilder Penfield's and Lamar Robert's *Speech and Brain Mechanisms*.[2]

---

[1]Bloom, B.S.: *Stability and Change in Human Characteristics*. New York, Wiley, 1964.
[2]Penfield, W., and L. Roberts: *Speech and Brain Mechanisms*. Princeton University Press, 1959.
See also Penfield's: "The Uncommitted Cortex." *Atlantic Monthly*, July, 1964.

Man, through electro-probing of the human brain, is beginning to understand something of its energy patterns and information processing. We apparently start life with a given total brain cell capacity, component areas of which are progressively employed in a series of events initiated in the individual's brain by chromosomic "alarm-clocks." Put your finger in the palm of a newborn baby's hand and the baby will close its tiny hand deftly around your finger, for its tactile apprehending organism is operative in superb coordination. Soon the "alarm clock" calls the hearing function into operation, and on his own unique schedule the baby will also see.

In a stimulating environment, the brain's chromosomic alarm clocks and "ticker tape" instructions inaugurate use of the child's vast inventory of intercoordinate capabilities and faculties. The child is not in fact taught and cannot be taught by others to inaugurate these capabilities. He teaches himself—if given the chance —at the right time. This provision of environmental experience conducive to the child's intellectual development has been termed the "problem of the match" by J. McV. Hunt, in his *Intelligence and Experience;*[3] he also speaks of "motivation inherent in information processing."

Bloom finds that environment has its greatest influence on a human characteristic—such as intelligence—during the period of time in which the characteristic is undergoing its greatest rate of growth or change. Thus, by age four, 50% of the child's total capacity to develop its I.Q. is realized.

If not properly attended to and given the chance to function, despite the brain's alarm clock inauguration of progressive potentialities in those first four years, the brain mechanisms can be frustrated and can shut off the valves of specific capacities and capabilities to learn, then or later on, in the specific areas. The capabilities need not necessarily be employed to an important degree immediately after being triggered into inception, but must upon inception be put in use and kept in use as active tools in the human

---

[3]Hunt, J. McV: *Intelligence and Experience.* New York, Ronald, 1961.
  See also his "Motivation Inherent in Information Processing and Action," in *Motivation and Social Interaction,* ed. by J.D. Harvey. New York, Ronald.

coordinating capability, else they will squelch themselves, "shut themselves off," not necessarily irreparably, but usually so.

Piaget has said: "The more a child has seen and heard, the more he wants to see and hear." I add: "The more a child has coordinated, the more he wants to coordinate."

By age eight, 80% of the child's total capability to self-improve I.Q. in learning how to learn is activated. By age thirteen, 92% of this capability is self-started into usability and by seventeen the final 8% of the total capacity to coordinate and apprehend, to comprehend and teleologically employ input data, has become operative.

Traditionally, the great bulk of government educational funds have been applied *after* the critical birth to eight period during which 80% of the child's educational capacity is being established. In the light of recent research findings, our input of personnel, funds, and energy into education must be reversed.* A powerful case can be made for inverting the educational structure—for paying the mother or other person responsible for the most important, formative years more than the college professor—in due ratio to her greater responsibility. O. K. Moore, of "talking typewriter" fame, has made a similar suggestion.[4]

Let us focus our efforts to help the new life on the critical first 13 years, when approximately 92% of brain function is progressively and automatically "turned-on," "tuned-in," "tuned-out," or "shut-off," in direct response to the positives or negatives of the individual's environmental experiences and potentials, keeping in mind that by age four is realized 50% of brain function, which must be properly set in use and kept in use.

Not only intelligence is developed during these formative years, but also the basic characteristics determining much of the individual's personality and behavior as well.

Will the older, adult life demonstrate that it really wants more

---
*Operation Head Start, Title I of ESEA and recent related programs appear to represent a more realistic utilization of resources.[5]
[4]Moore, O.K.: *Autotelic Responsive Environments and Exceptional Children* Hamden. Conn., Responsive Environments, Inc., 1963.
See also M. Pines: "How Three-year-olds Teach Themselves to Read—and Love It." *Harper's*, No. 1356, p. 61.
[5]"The Big Federal Move Into Education." *Time*, April 30, 1965.

life by designing an environment to foster the new child-life adequately—to nourish the unfolding flowers of the "cortical gardens?" As I predicted in the *Saturday Review*:

> In the next decade, society is going to be preoccupied with the child because through the behavioral sciences and electrical exploration of the brain we find that, given the right environment and thoughtful answers to his questions, *the child has everything he needs educationally right from birth*. We have thought erroneously of education as the mature wisdom and over-brimming knowledge of the grownups injected by the discipline pump into the otherwise "empty" child's head. Sometimes, parents say "don't" because they want to protect the child from getting into trouble. At other times when they fail to say "no" the child gets into trouble. The child, frustrated, stops exploring. It is possible to design environments within which the child will be neither frustrated nor hurt, yet free to develop spontaneously and fully without trespassing on others. I have learned to undertake reform of the environment and not to try to reform Man. *If we design the environment properly,* it will permit child and man to develop safely and to behave logically.[6]

The work of Bloom, Erickson[7] and others reveals that this environment must promote *trust, autonomy,* and *initiative*. The human newborn remains helpless longer than the young of any other species. It is *in trust* to the adult's competent care, and should experience no breach of basic trust.

The child needs to have an area that is really its own—just as individuals of other species need a minimum regenerative territory. The child's room should be his "autonomy area"—the new life's learning lab complete with the expendables needed for testing tension, cohesion, etc., by tensing and tearing techniques.

This leads into *initiative*—the third element of critically controlling importance during the first four years. Psychologists have long told us that the child needs to *touch* to get basic information, But he also needs to conduct all manner of experiments, as with

---

[6]Fuller, R.B.; "What I Have Learned: How Little I Know." *Saturday Review*, Nov. 12, 1966, p. 70.
[7]Erickson, Erick: "Identity and the Life Cycle." *Psychological Issues*. Monograph I, New York, International Universities Press, 1959.

gravity and inertia when he knocks objects off a table. Likewise, the child requires experiences which indicate the coherence of things. After tearing newspapers apart and finding they give poor tensional support he will want to explore silk and other materials. As W. Gray Walter has observed, "What the nervous system receives from the sense organs is information about differences—about ratios between stimuli."[8]

Children, first taking apart and then putting together, learn to coordinate spontaneously. They learn about the way the universe works.

Children mustn't be stopped thoughtlessly as they go through their basic explorations. If parents break up that exploratory initiative by too many "don'ts" or punishments, or by having things in the child's environment that are dangerous and by which the child gets hurt too frequently, his spontaneity will be stifled, probably permanently. Fortunately, a few determined and re-inspired individuals whose spontaneous employment of innate capabilities has been curtailed or abandoned due to childhood frustrations, manage to later "find" themselves, but these cases are rare.

In experimental work at Southern Illinois University, we have learned that the maturing student, like the younger learner, wants his privacy—his special place. We have developed a little individual, private room-booth with a windowed door which "belongs" to each student in our project. When he first enters he finds in his private "room" all kinds of desirable items: a telephone directly and privately connected to his teacher; a good dictionary; wall charts of the periodic table of the elements; a world globe; a wall-mounted chart of the electromagnetic spectrum; his private typewriter, and other items conducive to thought and study. It becomes an obviously realized privilege to be allowed to go into his private study, where his reflexes become progressively conditioned, by association with that environment, and he gives himself spontaneously to study, calculation, and writing. He finds himself producing. His mind really begins to work.

As S.I.U.'s President Delyte Morris—a true leader—has pointed

---

[8]Walter, W. Gray: *The Living Brain*. New York, Norton, 1953, p. 135.

out: "The assumption here is that 'dropouts' indicate inadequacy of the educational system and not of the human individual."

In my *Ideas and Integrities*,[9] I have said that education, in the sense of man's being *educente* (led out from) the monological fixations of ignorance, involves also being led into, *intro-ducente*, (introduced to) the new awareness of the dynamic fluidity of the infinite persistence of complex-yet-systematic interaction of universal principles.

I consider the primary concern of education as exploring to discover not only more about the universe and its history but also about what the universe is trying to do, about why man is part of it, and how man may best function in universal evolution. We are finding ways to help the child coordinate his spontaneous comprehension of the whole instead of becoming a specialist, without losing any of the advantages gained by yesterday's exclusive specialization.

Our present global civilization requires an educational approach embracing at the outset the most comprehensive review of fundamental "generalized" principles. As these are progressively mastered, the approach should continue through their subdivision and application to separate localized cases. Having established this order from "the whole to the particular" we need to take all of the advantages afforded us by the latest communications developments through which the complex patternings and behavior of universe may be brought within reach and made part of man's working everyday experience.

Today, the vastness, complexity and detail of our knowledge requires restructuring into assimilable wholes, to be imparted even at the most elementary levels in terms of whole systems. We can no longer think in terms of single static entities—one thing, situation, or problem—but only in terms of dynamic changing processes and series of events that interact complexly.

Despite their venerated status, a large part, if not all of our educational institutions and their disciplines are obsolete. Virtually everything man thought he understood concerning education is

---

[9]Fuller, R.B.: *Ideas and Integrities*. Englewood Cliffs, N.J., Prentice-Hall, 1963, p. 231.

fast becoming useless or worse. For example, because experiment invalidates most of the axioms of mathematics such as the existence of solids, continuous surfaces, straight lines, etc., much of the mathematical curriculum sanctioned by mathematical educators, adopted by school boards, and taught in all elementary schools is false, irrelevant, discouraging and debilitating to the children's brain functioning.

We are going to develop an environment in which the new generation is so protected from the lovingly administered nonsense of grownups that it can develop naturally just in time to save man from self-annihilation.

Half a century ago, in 1917, I found myself thinking that nature didn't have separate departments of Physics, Chemistry, Biology, and Mathematics requiring meetings of department heads in order to decide how to make bubbles and roses!

I decided nature had only one department and only one arithmetical, angle and frequency, modulating and coordinating system. I am quite confident that I have discovered an importantly large area of the arithmetical, geometrical, topological, crystalographic and energetically vectorial coordinate system employed by nature itself. It is a triangular and tetrahedronal system. It uses 60 degree coordination instead of 90 degree coordination. It permits kindergarten modeling of the 4th and 5th arithmetical powers, i.e., 4th and 5th dimensional aggregations of points and spheres, etc., in an entirely rational coordinate system. I have explored the fundamental logic of the structural mathematics strategies of nature which always employ the six sets of degrees of freedoms and most economical actions.

The omnirational coordinate system which I have named *synergetics* is not an invention. It is purely discovery. With the complete and simple modelability of synergetics it will be possible for children at home with c.c.TV documentaries coming to them, and making their own models, to do valid nuclear physics formulations at kindergarten age. With this fundamental structuring experience, and sensing through models, children will discover with experiments why water does what it does. They will really understand what a triangle is and what it can do and does.

I agree with Jerome Bruner, whose report of the 1959 Woods Hole Conference advanced the hypothesis that "any subject can be taught effectively in some intellectually honest form to any child at any stage of development."[10]

As Margaret Mead has indicated in her classic *Coming of Age in Samoa,* we must direct our educational efforts to preparing children for coping effectively with the choices and changes which are confronting them. We should design a *Curriculum of Change,* not merely a *changing curriculum.*[11]

Obviously, one of the reasons why scientific education has seemed too difficult for many is the fact that much of its mathematics is founded upon experimentally unprovable myths which must greatly offend the intuitive sensitivity of the lucidly thinking new life.

When we combine our knowledge that the period from birth to four is the crucial "school" opportunity with the discovery that entirely new mathematical simplicities are at hand, we must realize that educational theory is entering a period of complete revolution. Excepting the mathematical-physicists, the revolution about to take place in mathematics education may be amongst history's most violent academic *reforms.* You will not have to wait long to discover that I am right.

It is very clear to me that when a child stands up, breathing and coordinating exquisitely complex patterns by himself, gets his own balance and starts drinking in the patterns of cosmos and earth, he is spontaneously interested in coordinating the total information —the total stimulation. He craves to understand—to comprehend. That is why he asks his myriad questions.

New tools will make it easier for the young to discover experimentally what really is going on in nature so that they will not have to continue taking so much nonsense on experimentally unverified axiomatic faith.

Computers, suddenly making man obsolete as a specialist, force

---

[10]Bruner, Jerome: *The Process of Education.* New York, Vintage, 1960, p. 33.
[11]Mead, Margaret: *Coming of Age in Samoa.* New York, Mentor, Fourteenth Printing, March, 1962, pp. 144-145. See also:
Whitehead, Alfred North: *The Aims of Education and Other Essays.* New York, Mentor, 1951, p. 28.

him back into *comprehensivity* functioning, which he was born spontaneously to demonstrate.

Computers as learning tools can take over much of the "educational metabolics," freeing us to really put our brains and wisdom to work. A recent report by the President's Science Advisory Committee recommends that the government underwrite a program to give every college student in America access to a computer by 1971. I suggest that we give every preschooler access first!

One device I have invented to provide total information integration is the "Geoscope" or miniature Earth. After 16 years of experimentation and development, I can describe it as a 200-foot diameter sphere with ten million electric light bulbs—each with controllable light intensity—evenly covering the entire surface and hooked up to a computer to provide, in effect, an omni-directional spherical television tube which when seen at a distance, will have as good resolution as a fine mesh halftone print. The Geoscope, accurately picturing the whole earth, will be used to communicate phenomena presently not communicable, and therefore not comprehended by the human eye-brain relay. For example, we could show all the population data for the world for the last three hundred years, identifying every thousand human beings by a red light located at the geographical centers occupied by each one thousand human beings. You would then be able in one minute to develop the picture of the world's population growth and geographical spread trends of recent centuries. You would see the glowing red mass spreading northwestward around the globe like a great fire. You would be able to run that data for another second or two to carry you through three or four more decades of population growth. While the edge of the data would be unreliable, the gravity and momentum centers of population would be quite reliable. Or all the cloud cover and weather information around Earth can be shown and accelerated to predict the coming weather everywhere.

If we were to flash a red light for each one thousand "reading problems" in U.S. urban school systems, our metropolitan areas, including the nation's capital, would flicker in distress.

According to a March, 1967 *Washington Post*, "At least one out of three public school students in Washington is reading two grades or more below where he should be . . . Many are reading five, six, or seven grades behind."[12]

The question I would ask of the "reading readiness" advocates is: "When are these children going to be ready to read?"

In *The Case for Early Reading,* the authors have assembled considerable and convicing evidence that the preschool child [Why not call him the "school-at-home" child?] wants to and will learn to read at home *given the opportunity.*

Their argument that the "before age six" period is the *naturally* optimum time for language learning—reading included—is increasingly supported by recent research disclosures in diverse disciplines which, coupled with the historical evidence cited, merits the closest consideration.

Of current relevance is the March, 1967 *NEA Journal* report of the Denver study of 4,000 school children designed to determine whether beginning reading could be taught effectively in the kindergarten.

The experimental kindergarten group who were given special reading instruction 20 minutes a day and an adjusted program in the first and later grades showed the greatest initial and long-range gains in both reading comprehension and vocabulary. They also read faster than any of the other groups at the end of the third grade. Early reading instruction was shown, in short, to have "a positive, measurable, continuing effect."[13]

Stevens and Orem would agree that kindergarten as the time for introducing reading instruction* is preferable to first grade.

But, they argue, the *pre-kindergarten child* must be provided an environment which epigenetically enhances early reading, for he has the prime potential for language learning—a potential which, they say, will prove to be of revolutionary significance for educational strategists.

I am confident that these authors are going to win their "case,"

---

[12]Filson, Susan: "Reading Levels in D.C. Schools Shock New Teachers." *Washington Post,* March 16, 1967.

[13]Brzeinski, J., M.L. Harrison, and P. McKee: "Should Johnny Read in Kindergarten?" *NEA Journal,* March 1967, pp. 23-25.

*By "instruction" they mean informal, interesting, inductive, inner-paced learning. "Auto-education" is Montessori's term.

for it is increasingly evident that the child's neurophysiology is on their side.

What we must plan now, on an even more comprehensive scale than the important Denver project, are imaginative and innovative studies to determine the optimum school-at-home combinations of these elements: (1) home environment, with enlightened parents; (2) TV, computers and other tools and technology conveying the most cogent content, and (3) young child's motivation and sensitive period for symbol systems mastery—and communication-computational competencies.

Another device which I have invented to encourage comprehensive thinking is my Dymaxion map, originally published in *Life,* March 22, 1943, and the first projection system to be granted a U. S. patent as a cartographic innovation. Dr. Robert Marks has described it as "the first in the history of cartography to show the whole surface of the earth in a single view with approximately imperceptible distortion of the relative shapes and sizes of the land and sea masses."[14] This map, which I now call my Sky-ocean World Map, is an aid in effectively conceiving the totality of world (and universe) events.

Because three-fourths of the Earth's surface is covered by water, I have developed a "fluid geography" approach to the study of geography, to correct the "landlubber" bias prevalent in our schools.

I have also been engaged over the years in writing a comprehensive maritime reconstruction of history—a saga of the world's sailormen "seeding" civilization by ship.

When I talk about changing obsolete, ineffective and debilitating school patterns, the established reflexive conditioning of our brains tends to expect a lag of another 100 years to bring about that change. But the rate at which information is being disseminated and integrated into our current decision-making regarding the trending topics I am discussing indicates that the changes are going to happen quite rapidly. My advice to educators who are thinking about what they may dare undertake is,

---

[14]Marks, Robert: *The Dymaxion World of Buckminster Fuller.* Carbondale and Edwardsville, Southern Illinois University Press, 1960, p. 49.

"Don't hesitate to undertake the most logical solutions. *Take the biggest steps right away and you will be just on time!"*

The individual is going to study at home in his elementary, high school, and college years. Not until his graduate work days begin will he take residence on campus. Inasmuch as the period of greatest educational capability development is before age four the home is the primary schoolhouse—and kindergarten is the high school.

As John McHale, Executive Director of the World Resources Inventory has noted: "It is now literally and technically possible to have the equivalent of the school (or even college) actually in the home dwelling. This may very well be the indicated direction for educational and training development in the emerging countries. It is not really a new concept. The home/family dwelling as the prime educational environ and its re-integration as a fully advantaged unit are new."[15]

One may already "tune in" on knowledge through the radio, TV and telephone. With more sophisticated systems, now available, one may individually select, and follow through complex sequences and instructional programs.

Advances in educational technology have now made available a number of measurably efficient self-instructional programmed materials, which are swiftly developing into presequenced "packaged learning" devices employing video tape, film, book texts, plus the remote computer linkages via libraries and control centers.

As I have forecast in *Education Automation*,[16] we are faced with a future in which education will be the number one great world industry, within which will flourish an educational machine technology providing tools such as the individually selected and articulated two-way TV and an intercontinentally net-worked, documentaries call-up system, operative over any home two-way TV set.

In my 1938 *Nine Chains to the Moon*,[17]* I outlined a number

---
[15]McHale, John: *The Ten-Year Program.* Carbondale, Illinois, Southern Illinois University. World Resources Inventory, p. 79.
[16]Fuller, R. Buckminster: *Education Automation.* Carbondale, Southern Illinois University Press.
[17]Fuller, R. Buckminster: *Nine Chains to the Moon.* Philadelphia, Lippincott, 1938.
*Copies of the original printing (5,000) of this book are now a collector's item.—ED. NOTE.

of predictions including, "Broadcast Education: the main system of general educational instruction to go on the air and screen." Frank Lloyd Wright, reviewing the book for *Saturday Review,* agreed: "Dead right. The sooner the better."[18]

With two-way TV we will develop selecting dials for the children which will not be primarily an alphabetical but rather a visual species and chronological category selecting device with secondary alphabetical subdivisions, enabling the child to call up any kind of information he wants about any subject and get his latest authoritative TV documentary. The answers to his questions and probings will be the best information that man has available up to that minute in history.

The "lecture routine" which most teachers look forward to with as little enthusiasm as their students will give way at all levels to the professionally best possible filmed documentaries by master teachers with hi-fi recording. Southern Illinois University's film production division at Carbondale, in collaboration with independent producer Francis Thompson is completing a moving picture series on my *comprehensive anticipatory, design science explorations.*

While I confined my discourse to those unique aspects of my comprehensive thinking which provide pioneering interpretation of man's total experience as distinguished from the formally accepted and taught academic concepts, it required 51 hours to exhaust my inventory of unique experience interpretations and their derived patterns of generalized significance conceptionings. The 51 hours represented my net surviving inventory of unique thoughts which have been greatly modified and amplified by my progressive world-around university experiences.

(Over the years I have accepted more than 350 separate, unsolicited appointments or invitations to visit or revisit as a "Visiting Professor" or Lecturer at nearly 200 different universities or colleges in over 30 countries.)

Children must be allowed to discipline their own minds under the most favorable conditions—in their own special private environment. We'd better consider mass producing "one pupil

---
[18]Wright, Frank Lloyd: "Ideas for the Future." *Saturday Review,* September 17, 1938, p. 14.

schools"; that is, little well-equipped capsule rooms to be sent to all the homes; or we can design special private study rooms for homes. There are many alternatives but the traditional schoolroom is not one of them. I was invited by Einstein to meet with him and talk about one of my earlier books. I can say with authority that Einstein, when he wanted to study math and physics didn't sit in the middle of a school room "desk prison." That is probably the poorest place he could have gone to study. As does any logical human when he wants to truly *study,* he went into seclusion—in his private study or laboratory.

Much of what goes on in our schools is strictly related to social experience, which, within limits, is fine. But we will be adding much more in the very near future by taking advantage of children's ability to show us what they need. When an individual is really thinking, he is tremendously isolated. He may manage to isolate himself in an airline terminal, but it is despite the environment rather than because of it. The place to study is certainly not in a schoolroom.

The red schoolhouse—little or big—is on the way out. New educational media are making it possible to bring the most important kinds of experiences right into the home. With television reaching children in the privacy of their homes everywhere, we should bring education—school—to where the children are. This is a surprise concept—the school by television always and only in the home—if possible in a special room in the home. Ralph Waldo Emerson was right—"The household is a school of power."

TV is the number one potential emancipator from ignorance and economic disadvantage of the entire human family's residual poverty-stricken 60%. Even in the world's slums, TV antennas bristle. There is thus a wireless hook-up directly to the mothers and children who watch their televisions avidly. Whatever comes over TV to the children and parents is the essence of education, for better or worse. What is now needed are educational TV advancements of high order.

Photographs I have taken of my grandchildren (without their awareness) as they looked at TV illustrate the fabulous concentration of the child.

Give children logical, lucid information when they want and

need it, and watch them "latch on." Dr. Maria Montessori designed her "method" to tap the child's powers to attend and absorb.[19]

While great knowledge and ingenuity are being put into research on the channels through which education is conveyed, relatively little consideration has been given to *what* is conveyed in the communicated content. The magnitude of the task demands a most rigorous examination of "what" knowledge is to be imparted and in which *order, amount* and *forms* it is to be conveyed.

So the home is the school, education is the upcoming major world industry, and TV is the great educational medium.

All of this has been made possible by *industrialization* which I define as the extra-corporeal, organic, metabolic regeneration of humanity. Industrialization consists of tools, which, in turn, are externalizations of originally integral functions of humans. I divide all tools into the two main classes—*craft* tools and *industrial* tools. Craft tools consist of all those that can be invented and produced by one man starting and operating alone nakedly in the wilderness.

Industrial tools are those which cannot be produced by one man, such as the steamship Queen Mary, the giant dynamo, a concrete highway, New York City, or even the modern forged alloy steel carpenter's hammer, with electro-insulated plastic handles, whose alloyed components and manufacturing operations involve thousands of men and the unique resources of several countries of the Earth.

Words are the first industrial tools, for inherently they involve a plurality of men and are also inherently prior to relayed communication and integration of the respective experiences of a plurality of individuals. This is reminiscent of the scriptural account, "In the beginning was the word," which we may modify to read, "In the beginning of Industrialization was the word." Crafts are limited to a single man and involve only very local resources and very limited fragments of Earth and time, while industrialization, through the relayed experience of all men—permitted through the individualization of the spoken and written word—involves *all experiences of all men everywhere in history.*

---

[19]Orem, R.C. (Ed.): *Montessori for the Disadvantaged.* New York, Putnam's, 1967.

As I stressed in my keynote address to the 1966 Music Educators National Conference,[20] the *speech pattern of the parents* exerts a critically important formative influence during the child's early years.

If the parents take the trouble to speak clearly, to use their language effectively, to choose appropriate words, the children are inspired to do likewise. If the parents' tones of voice are hopeful, thoughtful, tolerant and harmonious, the children are inspired to think and speak likewise. If the parents are not parroting somebody else, but are quite clearly trying to express themselves, nothing encourages more the intuitions of the young life to commit itself not only to further exploration but to deal competently in coordinating its innate faculties. However, if the parents indicate that they are not really trying, or relapse into slang cliches, slurred mouthings, blasphemy, anger, fear, or intolerance, indicating an inferiority complex which assumes an inability of self to attain understanding by others, then the child becomes discouraged about his own capability to understand or to be understood.

If the proper books are on the family shelves, if there are things around the house which clearly show the child that the parents are really trying to educate themselves, then the children's confidence in family is excited and the children too try to engender the parents' confidence in their—the children's—capabilities.

The child's verbal ecological patterning is a fascinating process. My granddaughter Alexandra was born in New York. She was brought by her parents from the hospital to their apartment in Riverdale, just across from the northern end of Manhattan, which is quite a high point of land directly in the path of the take-off pattern for both of New York City's major airports, La Guardia and (now) Kennedy. The planes were going over frequently, sometimes every few seconds. There was the familar roar and, on such a high promontory, it was a fundamental event to a new life.

The interesting result was that my granddaughter's first word

---

[20]Fuller, R. Buckminster: "The Music of the New Life: Thoughts on Creativity, Sensorial Reality, and Comprehensiveness." Keynote address presented at the National Conference on the Uses of Educational Media in the Teaching of Music, under joint auspices of the U.S. Office of Education and the Music Education National Conference, Wash., D.C., Dec. 10, 1964. Published in the *Music Educators Journal:* Part I, April-May, 1966; Part II, June-July, 1966.

was not "Mummie" or "Daddy," but "air"—short for airplane.

How we see the world depends largely on what we are told at the outset of life before we unconsciously or subconsciously lock together our spontaneous brain reflexings.

The child can most easily learn to see things correctly only if he is spoken to intelligently right from the beginning.

As I was quoted in the *New Yorker* "Profile":

> I've made tests with children—you have to get them right away, before they take in too many myths. I've made a paper model of a man and glued him down with his feet to a globe of the world, and put a light at one side, and shown them how the man's shadow lengthens as the globe turns, until finally he's completely in the shadow. If you show that to children, they never see it any other way, and they can really understand how the earth revolves the sun out of sight.[21]

We are learning to test experimentally the axioms given to us as educational springboards, and are finding that most of the "springboards" do not spring, if they exist at all!

There is growing awareness that we have been overproducing rigorously disciplined, game-playing, scientific specialists who, through hard work and suppressed imagination, earn their academic union cards, only to have their specialized field become obsolete or by-passed swiftly by evolutionary events of altered techniques and exploratory strategies.

Biological and anthropological studies reveal that overspecialization leads to extinction. We need the philosopher-scientist-artist —the comprehensivist, not merely more deluxe quality technician-mechanics.

Artists are now extraordinarily important to human society. By keeping their innate endowment of capabilities intact, artists have kept the integrity of childhood alive until we reached the bridge between the arts and sciences. Their greatest faculty is the ability of the imagination to formulate conceptually. Suddenly, we realize how important this conceptual capability is.

Spontaneously, painters, dancers, sculptors, poets, musicians, and other artists, ask me to speak to them; or they look at my starkly

---

[21] Quoted in "Profile," *New Yorker,* by Calvin Tompkins, Jan. 8, 1966.

scientific structures, devices, and mathematical exploration models and express satisfaction, comprehension, and enthusiasm. The miracle is that the artists are human beings whose comprehensivity was not pruned down by the well-meaning, but ignorant educational customs of society.

Artists are really much nearer to the truth than have been many of the scientists.

In a beautiful demonstration, Gyorgy Kepes, of M.I.T., took uniform-size black and white photographs of non-representational paintings by many artists. He mixed them all together with the same size of black and white photographs taken by scientists of all kinds of phenomena through microscopes and telescopes. He and students classified the mixed pictures by pattern types. They put round-white-glob types together — wavy-gray-line-diagonals, little circle types, etc. together. When so classified and hung, one could not distinguish between the artist's works and scientific photographs taken through instruments. What was most interesting was that if you looked on the backs of the pictures you could get the dates and the identities. Frequently the artist had conceived of the pattern or parts in infra- or ultra-visible realms. The conceptual capability of the artists' intuitive formulation of the evolving new by subconscious coordinates are tremendously important. Science has begun to take a new view of the artist.

Philip Morrison, Head of Cornell's department of nuclear physics, talks about what he terms "right-hand" and "left-hand" sciences. Right-hand science deals in all the proven scientific formulas and experiments, while left-hand science deals in all of the as-yet unknown or unproven, that is, with all it is going to take intellectually, intuitively, speculatively, imaginatively, and even mystically, by inspired persistence, to open up the as-yet unknown.

We have been governmentally underwriting only the right-hand science, making it bigger and sharper. How could Congress justify appropriations of billions for dreams?

Pride, fear, economic and social insecurity, and the general reluctance of humanity to let go of nonsense in order vastly to re-organize are basic to the problem of education.

We adults must learn about our universe and how to modify the environment in order to permit life to operate an articulate the innate capabilities of man, the range and richness of which we are only beginning to apprehend. Innate cerebral and metaphysical capabilities have been frustrated by negative factors of the environment—not the least of which are the people in it who surround every individual. Today, the young people really want to know about things, they want to get closer to the truth, and my job is to do all I can to help them.

What I describe as *positive design science reformations of the environment* must now be undertaken with the intent of permitting man's innate faculties and facilities to be realized with subconscious coordinations of his organic process. *Reform of the environment* undertaken to de-frustrate man's innate capabilities, whether the frustration be caused by the inadequacies of the physical environment or by the debilitating reflexes of other humans, will *permit* humanity's original, innate capabilities to become successful. *Politics and conventionalized education have sought erroneously to mold or reform humanity, i.e., the collective individual.*

I have thought long and hard about architectural education and its potential for promoting environmental reform. I envision an utterly revised education of the architect, enabling successful students to operate on their own initiative in dealing both comprehensively and in effective depth in mathematics, chemistry, physics, biology, geology, industrial tooling, network systems, economics, law, business administration, medicine, astronautics, computers, general systems theory, patents and the whole gamut of heretofore highly specialized subjects.

This "comprehensivity curriculum" will prepare the graduating architects to gain the design initative, performing thereafter not as economic slaves of technically illiterate clients and patron despots but as comprehensivists, integrating and developing the significance of all the information won by all the respective disciplines of the specialized sciences and humanities, converting this information into technical advantages for world society in completely tooled-up and well-organized comprehensive anticipatory *livingry systems.*

When President Eisenhower was first confronted by the strategic data on atomic warfare he said, "There is no alternative to peace," without defining the latter or indicating how it could be secured.

Professor John Platt, Chicago University physicist and biophysicist, in a thorough survey of the overall shapes of a family of trend curves which comprehensively embrace science, technology and man in universe, said in 1964, "The World has become too dangerous for anything less than Utopia," but did not suggest how it might be attained. Jerome Wiesner, head of the department of nuclear physics at M.I.T. and past science adviser to Presidents Kennedy and Johnson, wrote in a recent issue of the *Scientific American* that "The clearly predictable course of the arms race is a steady downward spiral into oblivion."

So far, the only known and feasible means of arresting that spiral, by elimination of the cause of war, is the program of the World Students Design Decade."[22] This ten-year plan of world architectural students is divided into five evolutionary stages of two years each. Phase One, "World Literacy Regarding World Problems," was on exhibit in the Tuileries Garden in Paris, France, for the first ten days of July, 1965 (under the auspices of the International Union of Architects' Eighth World Congress). Emphasizing the central function of education and communication in overall planning, it dramatized the need for an informed world society to cope with the global nature of our problems.

It confronted the world with those basic facts leading the students to the research conclusion that human survival apparently depends upon an immediate, consciously coordinated, world-around, computerized, research marshalling and inception of the theoretically required additional inventions and industrial network integrations for the swiftest attainment and maintenance of physical success of all humanity.

Phase Two, "Prime Movers and Prime Metals," focusing upon the design of more efficient energy and metals utilization, was exhibited with the "Tribune Libre" section of the Ninth World U.I.A. Congress in Prague, Czechoslovakia, June—July, 1967.

There is a new dedication on the part of the world's young. Students are corresponding with each other all over the globe. These young people are about to seize the initiative, to help us make man a success on earth.

---

[22]For a listing of documents describing this program, write to John McHale, Executive Director, World Resources Inventory, Box 909, Carbondale, Illinois, U.S.A., 62901.

What I call "The Third Parent"—TV—is bringing babies half-hourly world news as well as much grownup-authored, discrediting drivel. The students in revolt on the university campus are the first generation of TV-reared babies. They insist on social justice the world around. They sense that imminent change is inexorable.

On Southern Illinois University's Carbondale campus, we are setting up a great computer program to include the many variables now known to be operative in world-around industrial economics. In the machine's memory bank, we will store all the basic data such as the "where" and "how much" of each class of physical resources; location of the world's people; trendings and important needs of world man, etc.

Next, we will set up a computer feeding game, called "How to Make the World Work." We will bring people from all over the world to start playing the game relatively soon. There will be competitive teams from all around Earth, testing their theories on how to make the world work. If a team resorts to political pressures to accelerate their advantages and are not able to wait for the going gestation rates to validate their theory, they are apt to be in trouble. When you get into politics, you are very liable to get into war. War is the ultimate tool of politics. If war develops, the side inducing it loses the game.

Essence of "success in making the world work" will be to make *every* man able to become a world citizen free to enjoy the whole Earth, going wherever he wants at any time, able to take care of all the needs of all his forward days without any interference with any other man and never at the cost of another man's equal freedom and advantage.

I think that the communication task of reporting on the computerized playing of the game "How to Make the World Work" will become extremely popular all around the Earth. We're going to be playing the game soon at S.I.U., and you'll be hearing more about it!

So, 1967 is the year of *The Case for Early Reading*.

Fortunately, the authors did not wait for "official permission" to use their initiative in exploring innovative approaches to answering the question: "When and under what circumstances should reading instruction begin?"

No one licensed the inventors of the airplane, telephone, electric light and radio to go to work. It took only five men to invent these world transforming developments. The license comes only from the blue sky of the inventor's intellect.

The individual intellect disciplinedly paces the human individual, who disciplinedly paces science. Science disciplinedly paces technology by expanding the limits of technical, advantage-generating, knowledge. Technology paces industry by progressively increasing the range and velocity inventory of technical capabilities. Industry in turn paces economics by continually altering and accelerating the total complex of environment controlling capabilities of man. Economics paces the everyday evolution acceleration of man's affairs. The everyday patterning evolution poses progressively accelerating problems regarding the understanding of the new relative significance of our extraordinarily changing and improving degrees of relative advantage in controlling our physical survival and harmonic satisaction.

In 1927, I gave up forever society's general economic dictum that every individual who wants to survive must earn a living, substituting instead a search for the tasks that needed to be done that no one else was doing or attempting to do, which if accomplished, would physically and economically advantage society and eliminate pain.

By disciplining my faculties, I was able, as an individual, to develop technical and scientific capability to invent the physical innovations and their service industry logistics.

Seventeen of my prime inventions in a wide range of categories have been granted a total of 145 patents in 56 countries around the world; incidentally, these patents in late years have produced millions of dollars of revenue. There are over 200 licensees, a number of which are industrial "blue chip" corporations, operating under these patents.

I've never had an "expert" who ever comprehended in significant degree the importance of any new development on which I was working. While this is deplorable, it's also understandable in the big corporations because research and engineering heads, confronted with something from the "outside," become very defensive, believing that acquiescence or approval would imply an admission that they are not alert themselves.[23]

1967 is also the year of Canada's World's Fair, EXPO 67; the United States Pavilion is a 250-foot diameter Geodesic Skybreak Bubble.[24] I invented the geodesic dome in 1947, and today can count over 6000 of my structures in 50 countries, ranging from play domes to the 384-foot diameter dome which rose in Baton Rouge, La. as the largest clear span enclosure in history.

A U.S. government citation describes "air deliverable geodesic structures" as the "first basic improvement in mobile environmental control in 2600 years." I can assure you I have never waited for any Bureau of Breakthroughs to grant me my permit to ponder, produce or prognosticate.

Forty years ago, after my pioneering studies had revealed the low technical advance in everyday dwelling facilities as compared with transport and communication developments, I invented my 1927 Dymaxion* House to function as part of my concept of an air-deliverable, mass producible world-around, new human life protecting and nurturing scientific dwelling service industry to transfer high scientific capability from a weaponry to livingry focus.

Children, born truthful, learn deception and falsehood from their elders' prohibition of truth. Much of this prohibition arises from a great, largely unconscious, parental selfishness born of drudgery and dissatisfaction (visibly rampant in the slums). The housing of children during their upbringing is the fundamental function of the home. If we solve the problem of the home, we can erase much of this unenlightenment.

The same year (1927), I published my conviction that two billion new era premium technology-dwelling devices would be needed before 2,000 A.D., requiring a whole new world-encompassing service industry. I predicted it would take 25 years to estab-

---

[23] *See* "Creativity Innovation, and the Condition of Man." A dialogue between R. Buckminster Fuller and Stanley Foster Reed. Wash., D.C., *Employment Service Review*, March/April, 1967.

[24] Jacobs, David: "An Expo Named Buckminster Fuller." *New York Times Magazine*, April, 1967.

*Dymaxion: The maximum gain of advantage from the minimal energy output.

lish that new industry. In 1952, right on theoretical schedule, the Ford Motor Company purchased the first of my large geodesic domes, which are the prototypes of the new era premium technology structures.

I anticipate that full scale industrialization of the livingry service industry will be realized by 1977, or just 60 years after the model "T" inaugurated the major world mass production industry. Henry Ford, Sr., pioneered the long-range world-around historical development of the application of the tools-to-make-tools system of mass production to larger end product tools, with his motorized road vehicle in 1907.

My structures, as reported in engineering and scientific publications, can cover very large clear span spaces more economically than by any other rectilinear or other shaped systems—for example, 1000-fold more economically weightwise than accomplished by the dome of St. Peter's in Rome, or 30 times more efficiently than by reinforced concrete.

The New York Herald Tribune in February 1962 reported that Dr. Horne of Cambridge University had announced, at a world conference of molecular biologists, the discovery of the generalized principles governing the protein shells of the viruses. "All these virus structures had proved to be geodesic spheres of various frequencies. The scientists reported that not only were the viruses geodesic structures, which latter had been discovered earlier by Buckminster Fuller, but also that the mathematics which apparently controls nature's formulations of the viruses had also been discovered (1933) and published by Fuller a number of years earlier (1944)."[25]

Although the words "genius" and "creativity" have been employed to explain my being "well known," I am convinced that the only reason I am known at all is because I set about deliberately in 1927 to be a comprehensivist in an era of almost exclusive trending and formal disciplining toward specialization. Inasmuch as everyone else was becoming a specialist, I didn't have any competition whatsoever. I was such an antithetical standout

---

[25]Fuller, R. Buckminster: "Conceptuality of Fundamental Structures." In *Structure in Art and in Science*. Ed. by Gyorgy Kepes. New York, George Braziller, 1965, p. 76.

that whatever I did became prominently obvious, therefore, "well known."

Luckily, as a special student at the United States Naval Academy in 1917, I had been exposed to a comprehensive educational strategy fundamentally different from the then-prevailing ivy league model. The potential I have since developed, every physically normal child also has at birth.

What, if anything, is hopeful about my record is that I am an average human and therefore whatever I have been able to accomplish also can be accomplished, and probably better, by average humanity, each successive generation of which has less to unlearn.

Man is beginning to transform from being utterly helpless and only subconsciously coordinate with important evolutionary events. We have gotten ourselves into much trouble, but at the critical transformation stage we are reaching a point where we are beginning to make some measurements—beginning to know a little something. We are probably coming to the first period of direct consciously assumed responsibility of man in universe.

Men sort, classify, and order in direct opposition to entropy—which is the law of increase of the random element—increase of disorder. Men sort and classify internally and subconsciously as well as externally and consciously, driven by intellectual curiosity and brain. Man seems to be the most comprehensive antientropy function of the universe.

Man, as designed, is obviously intended to be a success just as the hydrogen atom is designed to be a success. The fabulous ignorance of man and his long-wrongly conditioned reflexes have continually allowed the new life to be impaired, albeit lovingly and unwittingly.

Our most important task is to become as comprehensive as possible by intellectual conviction and "self-debiasing," not through ignorant yielding, but through a progressively informed displacement of invalid assumptions and dogma by discovery of the valid data. In this development, the young will lead the old in swiftly increasing degree. The child is the trim tab of the future. Let us respect in our children the profound contribution trying to emerge. The *Bible* was right: ". . . and a little child shall lead them."

As one who has spent his own lifetime comprehensively *putting things together* in an age of specialized *taking apart*—as a poet—I close with these lines—

> *And with Industrialization a uniformly beautiful*
> *world race emerges*
> *as does the fine chiseled head*
> *from the rough marble block*
> *certifying the god-like untrammeled beauty*
> *of a perfect human process*
> *implicit in the dynamic designing*
> *genius of the mind . . .*[26]

PROLOGUE BACKGROUND

The following Prologue contains highlights from a body of published and unpublished material of several thousand pages by or about Dr. R. Buckminster Fuller and his work: newspaper, magazine, and journal articles; books, manuscripts, and related documents; transcripts of lectures and addresses; and records of personal interviews, such as a six-hour interview with Dr. Fuller by R. C. Orem in March of 1967.

Responsibility for the selection and organization of material utilized and the form in which it is cast here, was borne, with Dr. Fuller's permission, by R. C. Orem, as were final writing and editing tasks. The elaboration of particular points and the exclusion of others reflect the editing made necessary by the remarkable scope, diversity, and quantity of material out of which the Prologue developed.

For a more extended treatment of the ideas compressed into these pages and of many other ideas which space limitations precluded touching upon, the reader is invited to consult the various works of the Fuller literature referred to throughout the Prologue.

---

[26]Fuller, R. Buckminster: "Untitled Epic Poem on the History of Industrialization." Jonathan Williams, Publisher, Highlands, North Carolina, 1962, p. 116.

PREFACE*

THERE REMAINS, however, one vital aspect of early teaching of reading which is too little understood. Bloom, at the University of Chicago, has pointed out that 50% of the growth in I.Q. takes place in the first four years. Studies of animal behavior cited by J. McV. Hunt, demonstrate that if deprivation of the opportunity for growth or the exercise of normal behavior is inhibited artificially by the experimenters, *the animals do not recover*. Studies of institutionalized infants with environments that are non-stimulating and poor in human relationships show deleterious consequences to the I.Q.

Bloom, summarizing these research projects and his own, makes it a central thesis of his work that changes in environment have greatest effect if they take place during the greatest normal growth. There seems no longer to be any doubt that the first five years or four are critical to the maximum development of the language, cognitive, and intellectual capacities of children. These are the decisive years.

Accordingly, language training up to and including reading should occur before age five, if the methodology is gentle, self-teaching, non-directive and paced to the development of each youngster. These are not impossible or remote requirements. Methods and materials to put such programs into operation are at hand now. We can no longer wait. *Our children at an early age need to experience the self-thrill of learning with success*. The inner satisfaction from learning to read at an early age is a powerful and dynamic force that will affect the whole future of a child.

---

*From—The well-documented case for teaching reading early. *Grade Teacher*, April, 1965, p. 92, By Dr. John Henry Martin, Supt. of Public Schools, Mt. Vernon, New York. Reproduced with permission. (Dr. Martin is now Vice President of Responsive Environments Corporation.)

INTRODUCTION*

A MAJOR TASK facing our society today is the achievement of universal literacy. Perhaps the most important dimension of this task involves teaching all children to read as efficiently as possible. Although reading instruction is at least 4000 years old, there is no agreement among experts as to how and when reading can best be taught. The numerous books on reading and the articles in the learned journals and popular magazines indicate that we are living at a time when the ability to read and the discovery of the most effective methods of reading instruction are matters of the greatest interest. In the past fifty years, there have been some 25,000 articles published concerning the teaching of reading. It is doubtful if any other single area of education has received so much attention.

There are at least two major reasons for our present concern about reading achievement and reading instruction: (1) To survive in a technological society, an individual must be able to read the various systems of symbols which are essential in our complex economy. (2) As a matter of record, our present educational institutions are failing to teach a significant number of normal children to read well. In 1960, for example, one authority estimated that one-third of the American adult public could not read above the sixth grade level.[1] Today, a number of studies indicate one out of three school children reads so poorly as to warrant special help.

Throughout much of United States history, and well into the

---

*Stevens, George L., and Orem, R.C.: A new approach to reading for young children. *Building the Foundations for Creative Learning*. New York, American Montessori Society, 1964, p. 170. "The hypothesis which we are going to present in this paper has three parts: (1) that language development is a unitary intellectual process which emerges out of the interaction of human intelligence and its environment; (2) that this process begins shortly after birth and is largely over by the age of about six; (3) that all avenues of language expression and reception, that is, listening-talking and reading-writing, should be introduced to the preschool child."

twentieth century, general literacy was not so critical a need. The poor reader could survive vocationally because there were many occupations which did not require much, if any, reading. Many of us alive today can remember a time when the blacksmith, the tailor, the farmer, or unskilled laborer needed only a minimum of literacy to function effectively in our economy. There was always a place for the man who was useful with his hands, however limited his formal education might be.

But this situation has been changing rapidly. Science and technology have revolutionized our social and economic institutions. First, mechanization and then automation have combined to create an economy in which the ability to read has become essential. Little more than a hundred years ago in this country, reading was a scholarly or clerical accomplishment; today reading is necessary to economic survival. There are today fewer types of jobs that do not require some reading; and, if present trends continue, there will eventually be none. Machines with electronic brains are replacing manual labor; and, by all indications, in the near future even menial tasks will require the ability to set dials and read instructions. It is only a matter of time until all aspects of our society are automated to some extent. When that time arrives, what will happen to the man who cannot read?

With this stark fact in mind, that a period is rapidly approaching in which virtually everyone will have to read with some degree of efficiency, let us consider the second point which we raised earlier: How well prepared are our schools to meet this challenge? Can we depend on the present educational establishment to teach "virtually everyone" to read well? In fact, how successful is our school system at present in teaching children to read?

Let us note the comments of those who have studied the problem. Albert J. Harris, educator and reading authority, wrote in 1962: "Roughly one-third of elementary school children are retarded readers, significantly below age and grade norms in reading skills."[2] Glenn McCracken, reading teacher and author of *The Right to Learn,* noted:

INTRODUCTION

> Can American school children read? Can nearly all of them read the subject matter of their various grades? Can most of them? The unequivocal answer to these questions is no. Measured by any standards in existence, the answer is no. . . . Our students cannot even read the textbooks that we, who know the limits of their abilities, write for them.[3]

In the same book, Doctor McCracken quotes statements of psychologists, school supervisors, principals, and teachers from all over the United States. The substance of their comments is that about one-third of our pupils are poor readers and, consequently, academic problems.

What happens to these students? The answer is a matter of record. Many of them do not last long enough in school to obtain the educational skills necessary to compete for jobs in our society. James B. Conant, internationally known scholar and former president of Harvard, has been studying American education for some years. In discussing our high schools, he notes: "I am convinced that a common denominator among unsuccessful school children who later become dropouts and perhaps juvenile delinquents is the failure to develop reading skills. Once these pupils reach the junior high school, it may well be too late to salvage them."[4]

The situation is indeed serious, perhaps grave, and the underlying causes are very complex. To perfect our system of reading education so that the vast majority of our citizens can learn to read with ease and accuracy will require years of research and study on the part of the academic and scientific community.

This book, *The Case for Early Reading,* is not presented as an answer to the reading question, for there is no single solution to the problem. But the book will deal with one important aspect of teaching children to read, that is, timing. When and under what circumstances should reading instruction begin? Whatever other factors may be involved, a clear answer to this question would be very helpful.

In order to determine the optimum time for introducing children to reading, it will be necessary to consider reading as a facet of a more general phenomenon—symbolic communication. Reading, seen in this context, is essentially the human capacity to communicate with symbols manifesting itself through the visual sensory system.

To anticipate a little, the subject of this book can be summarized in the following statement. Learned behavior, in many instances, is determined irreversibly by specific experience of the individual during definite periods of time, usually early in life and often of relatively short duration. These "critical periods" are found not only in areas of social and motor development but also in other areas of learning, such as language. Critical periods for learning are characterized by a greatly heightened capacity for learning, which if developed at the appropriate time, will produce a high level of proficiency in adult performance.

As an example, there appears to be a critical period in humans between the ages of one and five years for learning language. At present, we usually limit the child's experience during this time to spoken language symbols, but there is strong evidence that the same period of time could and should be used for the mastery of visual language symbols. This book will attempt to prove that learning to perceive aural symbols and learning to perceive visual symbols are neurologically and psychologically so closely parallel as to be almost indistinguishable.

The foregoing, if demonstrated, would indicate that children should learn to read at the same time and in largely the same way as they presently learn to talk. This would mean that reading should be introduced at home and in the nursery school in an informal manner, with no pressure on the child, in small steps over a long period of time and with extensive reinforcement from the environment. It does not mean that formal reading instruction, such as the child may encounter abruptly upon his entry into the regular first grade, should be introduced into the home or nursery school environment. For, in fact, it will be suggested in these pages that the abrupt and intensive program of reading instruction presented so frequently by teachers in crowded classrooms with limited opportunity for reinforcement is a chief cause of poor reading in our society. If we want our children to read with fluency and understanding, we must devise an environment in which they can learn to read as naturally as they now learn to talk.

The subject of this book is not a new method of reading instruction so much as a new way of looking at reading in relation to the whole process of language development in the child. It will argue that the visual reception of words (reading) is really only one expression of a more general power of the mind, the power to think symbolically. Language development is a unitary process which begins shortly after birth and is, under normal and natural circumstances, largely complete by the age of five. Therefore, all avenues of language reception and expression, aural-oral and visual-manual, should be introduced into the child's environment in an informal and functional manner.

REFERENCES

1. GRAY, WILLIAM: How Well Do Adults Read? *Fifty-Fifth Yearbook of the National Society for the Study of Education.* Chicago, University of Chicago Press, 1956.
2. HARRIS, ALBERT: *Effective Teaching of Reading.* New York, 1962, p. 338.
3. MCCRACKEN, GLENN: *The Right to Learn.* Chicago, Henry Regnery, 1959, p. 6.
4. CONANT, JAMES: *Slums and Suburbs.* New York, McGraw-Hill, 1961, pp. 56-57.

ACKNOWLEDGMENTS

The rationale for early reading certainly did not spring full-blown from a single individual's brow. Many persons over the years have contributed to the thinking regarding the theory and practice of promoting language development and early reading experimentation. The present authors have found journal references to early reading dating back to the 1800's. In addition to surveying the rapidly-increasing literature of early learning in general and early reading specifically, the present authors have had helpful discussions and correspondence with many individuals in various disciplines who are directly or indirectly interested in early reading. Of course, professional and public interest in the subject has recently increased tremendously.

Five years ago, to say that preschoolers could learn to read was something of a novelty, but now the tide has turned. In five more years, "early reading" will be a commonplace.

Among the many individuals whose work in reading and related fields, has, for the present authors, generated interest, inspiration, or insight, are the following. Mention of these individuals is not, of course, intended to imply that they necessarily endorse the viewpoints set forth in our text.

Dr. Dolores Durkin, who has done the most significant longitudinal studies of early readers to date; Wilder Penfield and his colleagues who provide a bridge between neurophysiology and the pedagogy of language learning; Nancy Rambusch, Lena Gitter and others who reestablished Montessori as a viable force in American early childhood education; J. McV. Hunt, William Fowler, B. F. Skinner, Omar K. Moore, Jerome Bruner and other psychologists who have devised ingenious approaches to studying the child's processing of information; each of the above-named has written significant, relevant books and/or articles of importance for the student of early reading; educators such as Arthur

Gates, Donald Durrell, and Glenn McCracken who have encouraged a new look at traditional "readiness" concepts; Charles Fries and other leaders in linguistics; Harry Harlow ("learning sets"); Donald Hebb ("cell assemblies," "phase sequences," etc.); Benjamin Bloom, author of a "landmark" book for students of learning; Konrad Lorenz and other "imprinting" researchers; Wayne Dennis and his colleagues studying infant learning; Martin Deutsch and his colleagues working in the field of cultural deprivation; Glenn Doman (*How To Teach Your Baby To Read*) whose work in neurological organization is an important contribution to the field of early learning, and Dr. Temple Fay; Helen Davidson, Lewis Terman, M. W. Brown, Winifred Stoner, authors of provocative studies of early reading; Austin Riesen and his colleagues in sensory deprivation work; J. P. Scott and many other researchers involved in animal learning; Jean Piaget and his colleagues; L. Vygotsky, brilliant Russian researcher of the mental processes; Arthur and Carolyn Staats; Lawrence Kasdon. In addition to the various professionals cited, the many parents who have taught their children to read, using a variety of approaches should be recognized; our wives and children helped us in many ways during the preparation of this book, and finally, and most importantly, we mention the preschoolers themselves. A relatively few learned to read in the past; many are learning presently; virtually all will learn in the future.

G.L.S.
R.C.O.

CONTENTS

Page

Prologue—Emergent Man—His Environment and Education, By R. Buckminster Fuller vii

Preface xxxiii
Introduction xxxv
    References xxxix
Acknowledgments xli

Chapter

One	LANGUAGE, MAN AND THE CHILD 3
	Main Points 3
	Summary 12
	References 13
Two	THE NATURE OF LANGUAGE LEARNING IN THE CHILD 15
	Main Points 15
	Summary 24
	References 24
Three	READING AND LANGUAGE DEVELOPMENT 26
	Main Points 26
	Summary 33
	References 34
Four	EARLY READING RECONSIDERED 35
	Main Points 35
	Summary 43
	References 43
	Suggested Readings, Briefly Annotated 44
	Additional Readings 46
Five	TOWARD A THEORY OF READING DISABILITY 48
	Main Points 48
	Summary 54
	References 54
	Suggested Readings, Briefly Annotated 55
	Additional Readings 57

Chapter		Page
Six	SOME ORIGINS OF PERCEPTUAL DIFFICULTIES	59
	Main Points	59
	Summary	64
	References	65
	Suggested Readings, Briefly Annotated	65
	Additional Readings	68
Seven	SIGHT AND SOUND IN READING	69
	Main Points	69
	Summary	76
	References	76
	Additional Readings	77
Eight	MONTESSORI AND EARLY LEARNING	79
	Main Points	79
	Summary	85
	References	85
	Suggested Readings, Briefly Annotated	87
Nine	RESEARCH AND EARLY READING	90
	Main Points	90
	Summary	102
	References	103
	Additional Readings	105
Ten	SOME ADVANTAGES OF PRESCHOOL READING	107
	Main Points	107
	Summary	115
	References	116
	Suggested Readings, Briefly Annotated	116

Appendix A—SO YOU WANT TO TEACH YOUR PRESCHOOLER TO READ SOME WORDS? ... 119
Appendix B—A PRESCHOOL READING PROGRAM ... 126
Index ... 133

THE CASE FOR EARLY READING

... I propose that the architectural departments of all the universities around the world be encouraged by the UIA to invest the next ten years in a continuing problem of how to make the total world's resources serve 100 percent of humanity through competent design.

>From—*The Architect as World Planner.* R. Buckminster Fuller's address to the Sixth Congress of the International Union of Architects.

Chapter One

LANGUAGE, MAN, AND THE CHILD*

MAIN POINTS

Marvel of the child's language mastery.
The child a limited creature by adult standards.
Three functions of language.
Nature of the language process.
Importance of language for mental development.
Serious effects of language deprivation.
Child's superiority in language learning.
Early childhood the "sensitive period" for language acquisition.
Timing and exposure crucial, not IQ or formal education.

IT IS GENERALLY ACKNOWLEDGED that between birth and about five years of age, every normal child will learn to speak the native language or languages in his environment. By about age five, authorities agree, this child will have substantially mastered the basic patterns of his language. Within the limits of his experience, he will understand and express basic ideas in his native tongue, and his grammatical expression will be functionally correct.

The quality and extent of language development in the child has been studied in detail by Dorothea McCarthy[1] and other authorities,[2] who have observed that the essential gramatical structure of language and a basic vocabulary are found in the speech of the five-year-old child. It is interesting to note that the vocabulary of the child of five, while difficult to measure exactly, may include several thousand words.

---

*Moore, Annie E.: The use of children's initiative in beginning reading. *Teachers College Bulletin.* Twelfth Series, No. 8. New York, Teachers College, Columbia University, 1920, p. 6. "The question may fairly be asked whether many children might not pass almost unconsciously into the art of reading, and largely by their own spontaneous effort, if they were surrounded by the right stimuli . . ."

The acquisition of language is a universal phenomenon which we have not only witnessed but experienced ourselves. In fact, we have become so accustomed to the rapid development of language in young children that we may give the matter little attention. We take the normal child's language proficiency for granted. Yet, students of speech and language development, who have studied the intricacies of the process, usually end by describing the young child's language achievement as little short of miraculous. For example, the noted philosopher, Alfred North Whitehead, said:

> The first intellectual task which confronts an infant is the acquirement of spoken language. What an appalling task, the correlation of meanings with sounds! It requires an analysis of sounds. We all know that the infant does it, and that the miracle of his achievement is explicable. But so are all miracles, and to the wise they remain miracles. All I ask is that with this example staring us in the face we should cease talking nonsense about postponing the harder subjects.[3]

In *Father of the Man,* a study of child development, Davis and Havighurst refer to the complexity of language and describe its mastery by the child as a feat of amazing virtuosity. Understanding, as they do, the limitations of the child organism, they marvel at the efficiency and ease with which he is able to absorb language from his environment.[4]

Let us consider the condition of the very young child. Physically, he is relatively uncoordinated; his immature central nervous system must learn to organize the perceptual experiences reported to it through his sensory apparatus; he has, initially, only limited experience upon which to build cognitively; he is dependent upon his environment for sustenance and safety. Above all, his intelligence, as measured by adult standards, is restricted. How then, one asks, could this rather helpless, incomplete human being accomplish with accuracy the mastery of a complex, abstract system of symbolic communication? This mastery, it should be remembered, occurs in the space of a few years, and without formal education.

Listen to the speech of a typical five-year-old. Note his ability to use present, past, and future tenses with substantial accuracy.

Observe that he has mastered the subject, verb, and object sequence in the active voice and can reverse the order to ask a question. Note especially that his speech is, in accent and grammar, a remarkably accurate reproduction of the language to which he has been exposed. By what educational process does the young child, who may still be learning to dress and feed himself, who cannot be trusted alone for long periods of time, become a fluent linguist?

McCarthy, in discussing the sophistication of the child's speech, hints at the magnitude of the child's accomplishment:

> This rapid development in such an intricate and distinctly intellectual function is indeed remarkable, when we realize that it occurs in individuals who are decidedly immature physically and who have the mental ages of only two, three and four years.[5]

By taking for granted this process, are we not ignoring an amazing feature of child development? May not this feature have important implications for educational practice and learning theory? As Whitehead suggested in his essay on education, if the child's mind can grasp the complex relationship between sounds and meanings, a purely intellectual feat, we should no longer persist in ignoring his obvious learning capacity and depriving him of other intellectual stimulation.

If we consider language in its broadest historical and cultural frame of reference, we discover that it serves three main functions. First, it is our chief mode of communication. Second, in various forms it is the repository for the accumulated wisdom, information, and technology of society. Third, as a means of identifying relationships and expressing levels of abstraction, it is man's most powerful tool.

Communication, as such, is not an exclusively human faculty. The use of sounds as a mode of signalling is shared by man with many animals. Mating calls, warning barks, distress cries and many other sounds are commonly used by certain subhuman animals as signals. Some of these animals can even learn to distinguish simple forms, use signs, and make limited abstractions. But no other animal, so far as research indicates, ever develops language in the complex form in which we find it among all cultures and races of men.

Only man appears to have the capacity for language development. Wilder Penfield, the noted neurologist and brain surgeon, wrote in *Speech and Brain Mechanisms:*

> When the child begins to speak, the animal is blocked and can no longer follow. This may be explained in part, perhaps, by the fact that man alone has an inborn control mechanism for vocalization in his cerebral cortex. Animals bark or mew or chatter by using neurological motor mechanisms in what may be called the old brain.[6]

Fundamentally, human speech is a system of mutually understood, arbitrary sounds which are used to represent beings, actions, and their relationships. This system of phonetic symbols, or code, can then be used to describe experience even when the ingredients of such experience are not immediately present. Though specific sounds vary from language to language, and may fluctuate within one language, all spoken languages are characterized by the use of sounds as symbols to communicate thought and feeling.[7]

Ogden and Richards, in their book, *The Meaning of Meaning,* develop the relationship between the symbol and that thing for which it stands. With few exceptions, the meaning attached to a given unit of sounds is conventional. There is no logical connection between the symbol and its referent. The only link binding the referent to the language system is the thought or idea which we have associated with particular sounds.[8] Men may use many different words to name the same blue sky.

Though the origins of language are still undetermined, there is little doubt that language is a function of man's central nervous system. We have already noted Penfield's observation that man alone possesses an inborn control mechanism in his cerebral cortex for vocalization. Furthermore, says Penfield, "The neurological structures required for another and much more important mechanism are probably missing, too, in the subhuman brain. That is the mechanism employed by man for ideational speech."[9] The human tendency to think symbolically cannot be separated from man's more general ability to grasp relationships and patterns. For example, most animals have some experience with falling bodies, yet only man can isolate, name, and speculate on the concept of falling as distinct from any particular object that falls.

Man's power to conceive abstract form is expressed in and complemented by his language symbols. For through the use of symbols man can pose increasingly abstract problems to his brain. Without symbols, man's thinking would be limited to noting relationships among immediate and rather concrete experiences. Between a falling apple and the law of gravity, there is quite an intellectual distance. If man had not been able to evolve symbols to express different degrees of generalization and abstraction, he could never have covered this distance. Philosophy and science are dependent upon the process of evolving symbolic constructs.

Finally, because man can relate and remember, he can transmit from generation to generation his accumulated experience. This process of accumulation and transmission of information through symbols has been the basis of human technical, social, and intellectual progress. The creation of symbols has enabled man to "raise himself by his boot straps." Language is the basis of socialization and education, for with language each generation has the opportunity to build on the foundation of past discoveries while recognizing and avoiding past errors.

Count Alfred Korzybski,[10] the founder of general semantics, called man the "time binder," for with language man escapes at least some of the bonds of mortality in preserving for posterity his wisdom. The "symbolic hoard" of a society and culture acts as a system of "cultural chromosomes." Successful patterns of living are transmitted by society through its oral and written traditions in a manner somewhat analogous to the germ cells maintaining the biology of the species.

No individual, however talented, could reproduce more than a fraction of the techniques and values which comprise the cultural endowment of his society. Children raised outside of society and denied the experience of a human environment become, in behavior, little more than animals. This is most strikingly demonstrated by the feral or "wild" children,[11] who because of desertion or other mischance become separated from their society. While reports on these children are necessarily anecdotal and uncertain, it appears that children who lack adequate exposure to human culture for long periods never fully recover from the effects of such experience. Their language development and other manifestations of human intelligence may be gravely impaired. This would indicate that what we have come to recognize as specifically human in the child is largely a product of early exposure to the values and concepts contained in the symbolic heritage of his culture.

There is at present a great deal of interest in a less extreme form of isolation, the phenomenon of "cultural" or social deprivation. The urban slum ghetto is a dramatic example of an environment which may operate to drastically limit a child's perceptual, language, and cognitive development.[12]

Also, research done on infants institutionalized in hospitals and orphanages has documented the fact that an environment which is insufficiently stimulating verbally and in other ways can have lasting detrimental effects upon the child.[13]

Language, or man's ability to organize his understanding of the world with symbols, is the most powerful tool he has devised. As Langer,[14] Cassirer,[15] and many others have recognized, symbolic thought is the clearest expression of human intelligence.

The child, in the act of acquiring language, is accomplishing his greatest educational task. As he listens, and strives to understand and imitate the patterns of sound which surround him, he is recapitulating the linguistic history of his race and society. But from an educational point of view, there is an element of perhaps even greater significance in the child's accomplishment. His evident capacity to master language during his first five years of life is absolute and final proof that even as an organism immature in many ways, the child possesses intelligence of a very high order.

This is not to say that the child possesses intelligence comparable to the adult's, but rather, that some mode of intellectual activity is in process in the language development of the child. Its form and nature of operation are little known at this time. Maria Montessori's fascinating book *The Absorbent Mind*[16] is the result of her work in penetrating the "mystery" of the unique mentality of childhood. Generally, students of learning have confined themselves to school-age children, adults, or animals. With the exception of the work of Piaget and a handful of other researchers, research done on thinking in young children has involved children old enough to communicate readily by speech. It is, of course, not easy to study thinking in a nonverbal creature, but eventually we must do so if we are to understand the primary stages in the evolution of learning in the individual. However, despite our lack of exact knowledge, it is possible to assert that the child has an intelligence that can learn complex systems of symbols. This capacity has very important implications for learning theory.

A further indication of the significance of language development in the child lies in the contrast between the child's and the adult's language learning. Looked at from a "commonsense" point of view, the adult should have every advantage. He already speaks one language, and has some insight into the structure of language. He has a wealth of experience. Moreover he has learned how to study and appears to be in every way the intellectual superior of the child.

Yet, interestingly, whereas the child learns a language rapidly, the adult does so only with great difficulty. Every year, thousands of young adults in secondary schools and colleges struggle with courses in language. Few ever master the language they study and most soon forget the limited vocabulary and few grammatical principles they worked so hard to master. While these young men and women are failing to learn a language, children in the country where the language is spoken are learning quickly and well that same language without the advantage of textbook or teacher.

Nelson Brooks, in *Language and Language Learning,* asks:

> If such a degree of control in the use of the most complicated grammar and syntax patterns can be attained by everyone within a space of four years at this immature age, how can one explain the strikingly lesser progress of students of a second language in our schools?[17]

Think of the thousands of adults of foreign extraction who have come to the United States and note how many retain obscuring accents even after living in this country for many years. In contrast, the children of these people have had no trouble in acquiring a native command of English when they have been exposed to it during their formative years. In addition, these children usually pick up a speaking knowledge of their parents' native tongue at the same time.

Certainly there must be some limit to the number of languages a normal child could master simultaneously, but history provides us with no instance in which a culture has exposed the child to a multilingual situation too complex for the child to master.

All of the foregoing evidence indicates that the child can learn language with greater facility than the adult, and that the child must have a special ability for learning languages, an ability which is largely gone by the time he is in school. Penfield has described the child's method of language learning as the "direct method." He notes that "the physiological reason for success in the home is that a child's brain has a specialized capacity for learning language—a capacity that decreases with the passage of years."[18]

Let us note once again that human language is a complex system of symbols representing concepts of varying degrees of abstraction, precisely interrelated, and capable of accurately expressing the ideational, esthetic, and value experience of human culture. Mastering human language is not simply a matter of imitating sounds or being conditioned to respond to certain stimuli with reflex oral behavior. It is no wonder that biologist Julian Huxley described human language as "the most complicated kind of skill in existence."[19] In mastering a language, the learner must understand that ideas can be organized with words or symbols which can in turn be communicated in the form of certain conventional gestures or sounds. As ponderous as the foregoing seems to appear, this is what is actually involved in the "simple" act by which a child points at a glass and asks for water.

The child's accomplishment in learning to talk, then, as has already been suggested, is an intellectual act. Moreover, since the child is able to best the adult in the attainment of this basic skill, we have some indication that the immature intellect has powers which will later be diminished if not lost. This is a point to which we will return later.

There is another aspect of the child's language aptitude which is worthy of discussion. Since all normal children become functionally proficient in one or more languages by the age of five, differences in native intellectual endowment do not appear to be critical determinants in the process. Of course very bright children, in a good language environment, make very rapid progress in learning to talk, but it is important to realize that even children of below average "IQ" can achieve a mastery of their native tongue by the age of five in a responsive environment.

While obviously there are significant differences in the intellectual potential of children, these differences, unless profound, are not sufficient to thwart the process of language development. Whatever the importance of IQ for school achievement, there is no indication that it is the significant variable operating in the mastery of language by the child.

We have, then, based on the universal experience of mankind, very strong evidence that the early years of life constitute a critical intellectual period for the learning of language. How or to whom a language is taught is not as consequential as when the exposure to the language occurs.

One might regard the young child's brain as a kind of computer with virtually unlimited capacity for recording and sorting impressions.[20] The brain will master whatever languages or dialects it is exposed to. If the child is exposed to Oxford English, he will speak with an Oxford accent. If the child is exposed to a Massachusetts or Texas dialect, he will reproduce these accurately. In other words, the child's language accomplishment is substantially a product of environmental circumstance. It does not matter to the brain which language, or which dialect of that language, it is exposed to; the brain will master it.

Moreover, the sophistication of the child's language development, or the lack of it, will also be largely a result of environment influence. If a child is brought up in a family where formal English is spoken, the child will speak with grammatical precision. Conversely, any child raised in a culturally deprived area will reflect in his speech the ungrammatical constructions which have been institutionalized in the popular argot of his environment.[21] Essentially, language facility is more the product of early, familial experience than it is the outgrowth of intelligence or education.

To review, every normal child goes through a critical period during which his intelligence is especially adapted to the mastery of symbolic language. Usually, this amazing learning facility is limited by environmental conditions to the acquisition of spoken language, but there is much evidence that this is a matter of historical circumstance, not neurological necessity. It is usual for the children of the deaf to learn the "hand language" of gestures just as naturally as most children learn to talk. We have already noted that the older child and the adult have difficulty learning new languages, and that the feral children suffer permanent language deficits. It is most probable, then, that this symbolic learning intelligence is largely a transient condition. This leads us to an important observation. Adults commonly assume, almost unconsciously, that the child's capacity to learn is inferior to their own. This notion is clearly false. The child's intelligence is not inferior to the adult's, but it is different. During its developmental stages, the human central nervous system is "programmed" to perform specialized learning tasks. In the accomplishment of these particular tasks, the child is superior to the mature adult organism. The ability to master symbolic systems is the clearest and perhaps the chief manifestation of this superiority.

SUMMARY

In this chapter, we have noted that language is at once the most complex and distinctly human of man's achievements. Its vital role in communication, cataloging of experience, and thinking has been cited. The considerable control which man has gained over his environment and destiny is made possible by his language development.

Normal children acquire language between birth and five with no formal instruction and in a natural, functional manner. After five, learning of language becomes increasingly difficult even for the most intelligent. It is apparent that the very young child has a language aptitude requiring a favorable environment and timing for its full realization. Feral, culturally deprived, and many institutionalized children may experience irreversible language and intellectual retardation.

Several lines of evidence were presented to illustrate the child's basic superiority in language acquisition over the adult.

There is implied in this situation pointed comment on our present educational practices. Despite the clear evidence of the child's superiority in language mastery, our society does not fully recognize the importance of the chronology of language learning for educational theory. The struggling students who fail to achieve any real competence after several years of language training could have, if exposed to that language in the pre-school period, become fluent. The acquisition of language is not a function of native endowment, academic aptitude, or educational methodology, so much as it is the result of developmental timing. Infants learn languages easily and accurately. The vast majority of adults learn only with great effort—and the results are limited.

It is vital, then, that all language experience considered essential to the fullest realization of a child's intellectual potential be introduced directly into the child's environment before the age of five. After that age, regardless of education or intelligence, the individual will be to some extent a language problem if he has been deprived of a verbally stimulating environment.

REFERENCES

1. McCarthy, Dorothea: Language development in children. *Manual of Child Psychology*, 2nd Ed., Edited by L. Carmichael, New York, Wiley, 1954, pp. 492-630.
2. Mowrer, O. Hobart: *Learning Theory and the Symbolic Process*. New York, Wiley, 1960.
3. Whitehead, Alfred North: *The Aims of Education and Other Essays*. New York, New American Library, 2nd. print., July, 1951, Copyright 1929, Macmillan, pp. 27-28.
4. Davis, W. Allison, and Havighurst, Robert J.: *Father of the Man: How Your Child Gets His Personality*. Boston, Houghton Mifflin, 1947.
   See especially Chap. 10, The mystery of language, pp. 107-116.
5. McCarthy, Dorothea: Language development of the pre-school child. Chap. VI, *Child Behavior and Development: A Course of Representative Studies*. Edited by R. Barker, J. Kounin, and H. Wright. New York, McGraw-Hill, 1943. pp. 107-128.
6. Penfield, Wilder, and Roberts, Lamar: *Speech and Brain-Mechanisms*. Princeton, Princeton University Press, 1959, p. 238.
7. Sapir, Edward: *Language*. New York, Harcourt, Brace, 1921.
8. Ogden, Charles, and Richards, Ivor: *The Meaning of Meaning*, 16th Ed., New York, Harcourt, Brace, 1949.
9. Penfield, Wilder, and Roberts, Lamar: *Op. cit.* p. 238.
10. Korzybski, Count Alfred: Time-binding and human potentialities. Edited by Ralph Hamilton, *General Semantics Bulletin*, no. 3, 1950, pp. 43-49.
    See also by Korzybski: *General Semantics*. Lakeville, Conn.: Institute of General Semantics, 1947.

11. ANASTASI, ANNE: *Differential Psychology: Individual and Group Differences in Behavior*, 3rd Ed., New York, Macmillan, 1958, Case studies of wild children. pp. 107-112.
12. RIESSMAN, FRANK: *The Culturally Deprived Child*. New York, Harper, 1962.
13. DENNIS, WAYNE, and NAJARIAN, P.: Infant development under environmental handicap. *Psychological Monographs, 71,* 1957.
14. LANGER, SUSANNE: *Philosophy in a New Key*. New York, Pelican Books, 1951.
15. CASSIRER, ERNST: *An Essay On Man: An Introduction to a Philosophy of Human Culture*. New Haven and London, Yale University Press, 2nd Print., May, 1962.
16. MONTESSORI, MARIA: *The Absorbent Mind,* 3rd Ed., Adyar, Madras 20, India, Theosophical Publishing House, 1961.
17. BROOKS, NELSON: *Language and Language Learning: Theory and Practice,* New York, Harcourt, Brace, 1960, p. 39.
18. PENFIELD, WILDER, and ROBERTS, LAMAR: *Op. cit.* p. 240.
19. HUXLEY, JULIAN: *Evolution in Action,* London, Chatto and Windus, 1953, p. 109.
20. FULLER, R. BUCKMINSTER: *Comprehensive Thinking*. Carbondale, Ill., World Resources and Needs Inventory, Southern Illinois University, 1965, p. 75.
21. OREM, R.C.: *Montessori for the Disadvantaged*. New York, Putnam, 1967, pp. 114-115.

Chapter Two

THE NATURE OF LANGUAGE LEARNING IN THE CHILD*

MAIN POINTS

Child absorbs language directly from environment.

Three conditions of adequate language exposure:
1. Clear presentation;
2. Repetition;
3. Consistently meaningful.

Four factors in child's language aptitude:
1. Impressionability of child;
2. Child's powers of imitation;
3. Child's "inventory memory";
4. "Plasticity" of his cortical substance.

An early stimulating language environment essential.

IN THE LIGHT OF THE FACTS that: (1) language is a complex tool of the human intellect and, (2) all normal children learn it by the age of five, let us examine the educational methodology which is responsible for such a remarkable accomplishment. What learning theory guides us in teaching our children speech? Where are the formal educational institutions which societies have evolved to insure that all of their offspring will learn to talk? One searches in vain, for under normal circumstances it is not necessary to "teach" a child to speak. There is, in fact, no accepted way of teaching the young child spoken language, and there is no educa-

---

*Stevens, George L.: A new look at early reading. *National Catholic Kindergarten Review*. Spring, 1964. "Research and theory from the fields of psychology, linguistics, neurology and physiology have impelled educators to take a new look at the intellectual development of the child from birth to six with particular attention to language development and reading."

tional theory which explains the exact process and progress of his language development. Children acquire language just by being exposed to it, at an early age and over some period of time. Children learn language by absorbing it. They learn directly and spontaneously from their environment.

McCarthy notes that "strikingly similar developmental trends are to be found in biographical studies from various countries regardless of the language being learned." This common developmental core in reports seems to indicate that "the process of language learning is essentially the same the world over."[1]

According to Kurt Goldstein, who has developed an "organismic" approach to language learning:

> ". . . Whatever language we consider, we observe, in the acquisition of sounds, the same sequence in time." [He cites Jakobson's confirmation of this in such languages as Swedish, Slavic, Russian, Czech, Indian, German, and Japanese.][2]

Language emerges in the individual, as in the race, long before formal education begins. In fact, as Edward Sapir[3] conjectured, language is most likely the ground out of which all culture evolves. Men had language for centuries before philologists, linguists, and finally semanticists began to analyze it. And today, after some years of study, the origin of language in the human race, and its somewhat parallel emergence in the individual, remain something of an enigma.

Although learning to talk is the major educational accomplishment of every normal human being and the sine qua non of most later intellectual growth, there are no pedagogical techniques or schools and little theory to explain the language process in its earliest stages.

Since children normally acquire language merely by being exposed to it during the early years of childhood, exposure appears to be the chief prerequisite for language development. This condition of exposure can, in turn, be broken down into three elements. First, the presentation must be clear. The child could not learn to talk well in an environment where everyone mumbled words or spoke rapidly. Because the child is unfamiliar with the sounds that make up words, most adults sense that it is necessary to speak slowly and clearly to the young child in the early stages of his speech development. A psychologist would say that the inexperienced brain requires a strong stimulus in order to develop a clear sensory image or memory. Long before the infant attaches meaning to speech, auditory images are being "imprinted" in the central nervous system, and these images become the foundation of speech expression and reception.

As Irving Lorge observed, research indicates that in the first year of life the child has the ability to utter any sound or pitch variation necessary to speak in any vernacular. As the human environment of the baby reinforces or rewards certain sounds or auditory images the brain operates selectively in the reception and reproduction of word-sounds. Lorge notes:

> Within a very few years the child will be able to utter reinforced sound patterns but may not be able to make the sounds that were never or rarely rewarded. For instance, Chinese adults may find it difficult if not impossible to say the "l" sound, substituting for it the nearly equivalent "r" pattern.[4]

Therefore, if the speech sounds of a language are not clearly imprinted in the immature brain, speech development will be handicapped. Although the exact nature of this "imprinting" process in language learning is not completely understood, Doty and Luria in *The Central Nervous System and Behavior* stress the importance of the mechanism.[5]

Secondly, not only must these auditory impressions be clear but, as has been suggested, they must be repeated frequently over some period of time. All learning requires some degree of reinforcement or repetition to become permanent in a neural trace or engram in the brain. Mothers "instinctively" sing and talk to their infants. The normal baby has hours of daily exposure to speech sounds.

The importance of this is indicated by the sluggish language development of institutionalized children who do not receive a normal amount of parent-surrogate language stimulation. Goldfarb,[6] Dennis and Najarian among others,[7] have studied the effect of a deprived language environment on the development of speech. In general, it has been determined that foundling children reared without the normal social stimulation of language play from a parent or surrogate are, subsequently, retarded in language and intelligence. From these studies it appears that an infant needs extensive interaction with an adult in order to develop the rudiments of language.

Third, the word-sounds to which the child is exposed must be made meaningful by association with their objects of reference. This means that the words must be presented to the child in such a way that they are clearly paired with specific persons, objects, or actions. This occurs quite naturally in the normal environment. Words are used in the same context over and over again, and children quickly learn to associate names with particular people, objects, and actions.

Where these three conditions of exposure are met, the brain of the infant seems able to absorb language out of its environment. Therefore, although no one can yet identify all of the factors involved in the child's mastery of language, we are able to state that it is evident there must be a critical stage of language sensitivity which characterizes all normal children, and which enables them to learn language rapidly and naturally. As Norbert Wiener aptly noted in his classic, *The Human Use of Human Beings,*[8] children possess a language aptitude between birth and about six years of age. After this age the aptitude seems to decline rapidly and by the teens, most children find the acquisition of language very difficult.

We have here what seems to be a unique learning situation, for with language neither maturation nor the inherited level of intelligence are the chief factors. The important condition, we have concluded, is adequate exposure at the appropriate level of development. With language, we do not ask if the child is old enough, but rather if he is young enough! In teaching language, the educator should not ask if the child is "ready" to learn but rather, he should ask if it is too late to teach him.

From the point of view of educational theory, it is of great importance to note that as the child is advancing in knowledge and skills in so many other areas, in language aptitude he is steadily declining. This developmental paradox suggests that educational theory which only focuses upon the unfolding of human potential through maturation and experience, which arbitrarily assumes that the child is in every way inferior to the adult—is inadequate to explain the phenomenon of language development in the normal child.

For, in point of fact, the child is superior to the adult in the facility of language mastery. No adult will ever match the direct and rapid skill with which the infant masters language. However superior the adult mentality may be to the child's, there remains the language area, in which the child has a kind of "neurological" advantage.

In passing, let us mention an ancillary notion derived from this general principle. The verbal facility of the child is not merely a result of his genetic endowment, but is also a product of the amount of time he spends in the company of articulate adults. The effects of environmental exposure are inextricably interwoven with those of heredity. This has been substantiated by recent work done with the socially disadvantaged children of the urban slums. Many of these children enter school with such a limited language background that they are subject to what Deutsch and his colleagues have termed a "cumulative deficit phenomenon."[9] That is, lower-class Negro and white children, compared with their middle-class peers not only do not catch up scholastically but fall ever-farther behind until, by grade five or six, the deprived youngster is a confirmed failure. One strategy for attacking this problem, according to those who have studied this problem, is to send these children to nursery school where they can get the needed language experience in their critical period of development.[10]

Let us examine some other features of the child's language development, for although the exact nature of language acquisition in the infant is not yet known, there are certain characteristics of the immature brain which are understood and which shed some light on the language aptitude of the child.

First, the young child is very impressionable, and experiences which occur during early years are the most lasting in effect. This notion of the role of formative factors is not new. The contemporary school of psychoanalytic human development is based to a large extent on the assumption that the early years of life constitute a critical period for affectional "imprinting." The predominant, Freudian theory of human behavior holds that early interpersonal encounters cathect the child's libido or life force and limit, through unconscious structures, the adult's capacity for self direction and expression.[11] And, although this theory concerns itself largely with the emotional facet of human development, it can be inferred that similar consequences may attend the child's intellectual growth.

The child reared in an articulate family circle, where sophisticated language and esthetic interest are woven into the fabric of family life will reflect these influences. James Joyce, in his autobiographical novel, has left an historical record of the birth of his own dissonant, verbal talent. In reading *Portrait of the Artist as a Young Man*,[12] one cannot help but feel that the verbal polemics which were a part of Joyce's early experience were a factor in producing his own fluency with words, (as well as his disenchantment with man).

Men have always described the period of childhood as the "formative years," that period during which outside influences have their greatest impact. The permanent and pervasive nature of early language experience is related to this more general phenomenon.

Secondly, the very young child is known to have unusual powers of imitation. The child appears to have a special gift of mimicry. He reproduces with fidelity the values, attitudes, and mannerisms of the adults with whom he comes in contact. This tendency to imitate is reflected in the speech of young children, for all children "imitate" the language of their environment. In discussing language McCarthy has commented:

> Most observers of child development report a tendency to imitation in all functions and that this tendency is readily observed in the reproduction of vocal sounds. Many writers regard this imitative tendency as the most important single factor in the acquisition of language by the child.[13]

Third, all children appear to have special powers of memory and though the exact nature of these powers is not known, in general it seems that infants manifest a type of "inventory memory." This faculty has been called "eidetic imagery" by the psychologists who have studied it.[14] The child appears to have the power to reexperience a sensory stimulus in precise and vivid detail. Shown a picture, some of the children tested have been able to describe it in minute detail hours or even months later. Allport has suggested that this eidetic imagery enables the brain to elaborate sensory experience, and through this repetition perfect its own perceptual and adaptive responses. Even though the function of this special memory aptitude in babies is not completely understood, it is clearly related to the child's language faculty and like that faculty tends to diminish after five years of age.[15]

Fourth, let us note certain facts from developmental neurology which reinforce our concept of the child's special learning faculties. Between birth and five, the brain undergoes growth and change at a great rate of speed. By about four or five the brain practically stops growing in magnitude.[16] Neurologists feel that those experiences to which the brain is subjected during this early period are of great and lasting effect, for while the brain is in the process of forming itself, experiences tend to leave permanent traces in the cell structures; these traces, in turn, affect later experiences. It would appear that early experiences "imprint" themselves in some manner on the physical substance of the nerve cells in the brain, and that these imprintings become a permanent part of the organism.[17]

An example of this which is quite common and related to our subject is that of language accent. For, as we have noted, while the young child can imitate the accents of one or two languages in his environment, the adult usually pronounces a new language with the accent of his native tongue. Even in those rare instances where an adult masters a new language and has no apparent accent, there seem to be important differences between the native and the second tongues. Though the listener may not be able to detect any accent in the second language, certain stress situations will reveal the superficial nature of the later acquisitions.

Joseph Conrad, the English novelist, was Polish by birth and spoke Polish and French as a child. In his youth, he mastered English and spoke it as a native. As a man, he became famous for his English style. It appeared that he had perfect mastery of English in both writing and speaking. Yet as he grew older his speech was increasingly blurred by an accent; and in later illnesses, his English became mixed with Polish even though no one in his household spoke the latter language. Polish, the language he learned before five, was still most deeply rooted in his mind; and, under the stress of degeneration of the nervous system and illness, this "imprinted" language emerged and dominated his speech. Conrad's case is by no means isolated, for the same return to the language and imagery of childhood is typical of the aged and of stroke victims with aphasia.

A native language can only be acquired in childhood, for the brain of the adult has passed beyond the plastic stage and cannot acquire the sound images of language as permanent impressions. Older language sounds learned in the critical period tend to dominate or interfere with the adult's attempts to imitate the sounds of the new language. It is evident that there is a phase of brain maturation during which perceptual imagery of speech sounds can readily be imprinted, but after this phase passes new images tend to be interpreted as variations of the primary image.

Any human brain which is not sufficiently exposed to language in the formative period (the "preschool" years) will be, to some extent, retarded.

Wiener comments, ". . . if speech is not learned at the proper time, the whole social aspect of the individual will be aborted."[18] This means that the human brain must be exposed to certain experiences at certain times in order for its full potential to be realized. For example, verbal intelligence depends largely on early exposure to language. If a child has little or no language experience during the first five or six years of life, his potential for education will be limited. In other words, if Shakespeare had been raised outside of a human language environment during much of his formative period, not only would he have never written his great poems and plays, but it is very likely he would never have learned to speak fluently. His native genius would have been lost as a consequence of a deprived language environment.

If one is going to acquire a language in the fullest sense and in the most natural way, one must start while still an infant. Our system of language instruction in the school is at cross purposes with nature, which designed man with a built-in language aptitude in his early childhood.[19]

Let us review, then, the four learning qualities which characterize the language development of the very young child. First, he is at his most psychologically impressionable stage, and his early language experience will always be the most meaningful to him emotionally. The songs and sayings of his native tongue will most move him, and the poetry of his native tongue will be with him to death. No subsequent language, however thoroughly mastered, will ever have the same power over his attitudes and feelings.

Second, he has at this time a natural disposition to imitate the actions, attitudes and speech of the people in his world. With little experience of his own, the child naturally tries to match the patterns of actions and words surrounding him. The speed and accuracy with which he is able to accomplish this imitation is truly amazing, for no adult ever rivals a child in this art of mimicry. To well-educated American Army officers, the word sounds of Japanese house servants were hard to distinguish and almost impossible to reproduce, but their young offspring, playing with the children of the Japanese house servants, soon spoke with a native accent.

Third, children have extraordinary powers of memory for detail. Whereas adults tend to remember in general outline, the young child can reproduce mentally the exact sights and sounds of his environment. In the process of language mastery this special faculty must function as a kind of tape recorder. The infant's brain appears to play back over and over again sounds to which it has been exposed. And while these sounds are not necessarily consciously of great significance to the child, they are the basis for language development. Almost from birth, the child's brain begins to "drink in" these auditory "images" of sounds—sound images which through external and internal repetition become permanently imprinted in the neural network of the central nervous system.

Fourth, the physical makeup of the immature brain cells provides a kind of special sensitivity to experience. The immature central nervous system is plastic and in process of formation. The course and, to some extent, quality of its development will depend upon the experiences to which it is exposed in this growing stage. This fourth factor is the physiological counterpart of the other three characteristics of the immature human intellect. Taken together, these four general factors, which overlap, of course, constitute the child's language aptitude. It is this special state, existing only during a certain stage of development in the human organism, which explains the special language aptitude of the child.

In both learning theory and educational practice we have not yet fully acknowledged the transitory nature of the child's sensitive period for language with a view to exploiting this period pedagogically before it has passed beyond recovery.

SUMMARY

In this chapter, we have discussed further the critical role of early language experience in the development of the child, and have suggested that it is most pertinent to examine the process by which the young child acquires his language. Specifically, it is of great importance to study the conditions which are prerequisite for the child's mastery of language. Since every normal human being goes through a period of special language sensitivity, any consideration of the essential features and circumstances of that learning stage could provide important insights into the nature of the learning process in general.

In examining the conditions under which the child learns to talk, we find that, given a minimum of innate capacity, only exposure is essential. Exposure is comprised of experience that is clear, repetitive and consistently meaningful. These are the only educational prerequisites the normal brain seems to require in order to master one or more languages.

The young child's language aptitude seems to be a product of at least four factors: the impressionability of the infant's mind; the special power of eidetic imagery or memory possessed by young children; their amazing imitative ability; and the plasticity of the growing central nervous system.

The child's proficiency in language acquisition leads us to recommend a reversal of much traditional educational philosophy and practice, for in the mastery of language it is inexperience and immaturity which constitute the ground for the functioning of a kind of special intelligence or language aptitude. Maturation and formal education limit the brain's capacity to absorb language directly.

REFERENCES

1. McCarthy, Dorothea: Language development in children. *Manual of Child Psychology*. 2nd Ed., Edited by L. Carmichael, New York, Wiley, 1954, p. 577.
2. Goldstein, Kurt: *Language and Language Disturbances*. New York, Grune & Stratton, 1948, p. 36.

3. SAPIR, EDWARD: *Language.* New York, Harcourt, Brace, 1921.
4. LORGE, IRVING: *Teachers College Record,* 57, Nov. 1955, p. 76.
5. DOTY, ROBERT, and LURIA, ALEXANDER: In the discussion following Verbal regulation of behavior, by Alexander Luria in *The Central Nervous System and Behavior.* Transactions of the Third Conference, Feb. 21-24, 1960, Princeton, N.J., Edited by Mary Brazier, New York, Josiah Macy, Jr., Foundation, 1960, p. 379.
6. GOLDFARB, W.: Effects of early institutional care on adolescent personality. *Journal of Experimental Education, 12*:106-129, 1943.
7. DENNIS, W., and NAJARIAN, PERGROUHI: Infant development under environmental handicap. *Psychological Monographs, 71,* 1957.
8. WIENER, NORBERT: *The Human Use of Human Beings: Cybernetics and Society.* Boston, Houghton Mifflin, 1950, See Chap. IV, The mechanism of language, especially p. 95.
   See, PENFIELD, WILDER, and ROBERTS, LAMAR: *Speech and Brain-Mechanisms.* Chap. XI, Epilogue—the learning of languages, pp. 235-257.
9. DEUTSCH, MARTIN: The role of social class in language development and cognition. *American Journal of Orthopsychiatry. 35*:78-88, 1955.
10. OREM, R.C.: (Ed.) *Montessori for the Disadvantaged.* New York, Putnam, 1967.
11. HILGARD, ERNEST: *Theories of Learning.* 2nd Ed., New York, Appleton-Century-Croft, 1956, pp. 290-327.
12. JOYCE, JAMES: *Portrait of the Artist as a Young Man.* New York, Viking, 1964.
13. MCCARTHY, DOROTHEA: Language development. *A Handbook of Child Psychology,* 2nd Ed., Worcester, Mass., Clark University Press, 1933, pp. 338-339.
14. ALLPORT, GORDON W.: Eidetic imagery. *British Journal of Psychology, 15*:99-120, 1924.
15. KLUVER, HEINRICH: Eidetic imagery. *A Handbook of Child Psychology.* 2nd Ed., Worcester, Mass., Clark University Press, 1933, pp. 699-722.
16. TANNER, J.M.: Physical and physiological aspects of child development. First Discussion in *Discussions on Child Development,* Edited by J. M. Tanner and Barbel Inhelder, Vol. 1, New York, International Universities Press, 1953, p. 38.
17. MOLTZ, HOWARD: Imprinting: empirical basis and theoretical significance. *Psychological Bulletin, 57*:291-314, 1960.
18. WIENER, NORBERT: *Op. cit.,* p. 95.
19. BROOKS, NELSON: *Language and Language Learning: Theory and Practice.* See Chap. 3, Mother tongue and second language, pp. 33-42.

Chapter Three

READING AND LANGUAGE DEVELOPMENT*

MAIN POINTS

Why not reading learned "naturally"?
Language as the interpretation of neural patterns.
Codes and sensory modalities secondary in language.
Language a function of the brain.
Only the brain can learn.
Reading a central process.
Human communication a complex transactional process.
All sensory input electro-chemical.
The "crosstalk" of synesthesia.
Equivalency of sensory modalities in language.

I F, AS ALL EVIDENCE INDICATES, the very young child has an aptitude for language mastery, one which has begun to wane after five, could not this same aptitude or special talent be utilized in the learning of reading? If the proper environmental circumstances were provided, could not the child learn to read as naturally as he learns to listen and talk? This suggestion is not new, for Anderson and Dearborn in their *Psychology of Teaching Reading,* (1952) made a similar conjecture. After pointing out that children require no "special tutelage" in the process of learning to talk, they suggest that children might also learn to read in much the same "natural fashion that they earlier learned to talk."[1]

This proposition may, at first glance, seem fantastic, but is it any more fantastic than the actual fact of the child's mastery of

---

*Orem, R.C.: Preschool patterning and language learning. *National Catholic Kindergarten Review,* Spring, 1966. "The very young child has a general aptitude for language—spoken and written—which should be exploited. The brain that can process spoken words can process printed ones, given a clear, strong, consistent signal."

spoken language? For, if the child by age five can understand and reproduce all the basic language forms of adult speech, would it not be reasonable to assume that he could approximate the same feat with visual language, given the appropriate conditions?

Arthur Gates, professor of education at Teachers College, Columbia University for many years, made this same point in 1954. Gates saw the close parallel between aural and visual language:

> Psychologically there is little difference between learning, as it were, to "read" spoken words and learning to read printed words. Spoken words come to the child through sound waves, and printed words through light waves. The main reason they learn to understand spoken words first is merely that it is more convenient for parents and others to use them than to present printed material.[2]

If the child can learn to recognize and create the complex patterns of sounds we call speech, why could he not be taught to recognize the patterns of letters we call writing? Let us remember that language is essentially a function of human intelligence. The language aptitude of the child is in the central nervous system. It is not in the ears, vocal cords, eyes or hands, for these are only "instruments" of the human intellect. Language is a central process of the brain, and sensory and motor faculties are only the vehicles of reception and expression. There is nothing in the retina of the eye which can learn to read and there is nothing in the hand which can master writing.

Knud Hermann, the Danish neurologist, in his *Reading Disability: A Medical Study of Word-blindness and Related Handicaps*,[3] stresses the fact that many superior readers actually suffer from minor visual anomalies such as myopia or strabismus, but that these "visual faults" do not appear to block the effectiveness of their reading. Hermann concludes that this is so because reading is not primarily a sensory process but a central one. He notes that it is the human central nervous system which learns to read.

The ear can not think nor can it remember. The ear is an aural receptor with no capacity to learn. It can only pick up patterns of sound for transmission to the brain. The sounds have no meaning until they reach the brain. There is nothing about the human ear which gives it any aptitude for language. In fact, many animals have more acute hearing than that possessed by people. Dogs, for instance, can hear sounds of a much higher pitch than can human beings but no matter how superior their auditory faculty may be, dogs never master speech. The human brain alone seems able to build up complex patterns of association between sounds and objects or actions, and to then treat the sounds as symbols representing the objects or actions. The mechanics of hearing and talking, then, are not the essence of the language process. In the acquisition of speech, the ear has only one function, which is to report clearly the forces which impinge upon it.

Most animals have their own system of cries and calls which make up a crude language, but it is only the human brain which has been able to organize these sounds into an "abstract" language. Studies on the talking birds, parrots, jays, and others have shown that however extensive their vocabularies may be, their words do not have the symbolic function of human speech.[4] The verbal responses of these birds are never meaningful in the absence of the conditioning stimuli.

Normal children learn to speak simply by being exposed to consistent patterns of sounds associated with objects and actions. In other words as long as the lines are open, and the brain is getting a clear, strong, consistent signal, it will be able to record and organize sounds into their language forms. Throughout human history, men have acquired their native language through this simple exposure. The only concession which parents have made to the child's brain is to speak somewhat more slowly and clearly to the child, to assure that the brain receives adequate signals. Beyond this, all that is required is repetition, through which the child comes to associate the sound and the object.

The language aptitude as such exists in the brain, for as we have pointed out, the senses only transmit experiences to the brain in the form of nerve impulses. It is the brain which interprets these patterns of neural impulses from the ear and eye as sounds and sights. Moreover, these impulses are electro-chemical in nature and as far as is known, of the same basic form when they reach the brain. All sensory input involves the same kind of neural transmission whether it comes from the eye, ear, sense organs of touch or the other senses. The brain distinguishes these sensory inputs at their destination. Strange as it may seem, at first, there are no sound waves or light waves in the brain, but only patterns of neural stimulation which are differentiated in the cerebral cortex.

This fact is most clearly demonstrated by the phenomenon of synesthesia. In this situation, sensory information from one nerve pathway crosses into another and as a result, sound, for example, may be confused with sight. This is called synopsia, ". . . a type of synesthesia in which visual sensations are closely associated with auditory sensations and appear regularly whenever the latter are stimulated."[5] A particularly interesting case of synopsia was reported by H. S. Langfeld. This subject responded to the notes of the chromatic scale with color sensations. Each note of the scale evoked in the mind of the subject a particular color. The colors remained consistent and were the same when tested some seven years later.[6]

W. Gray Walter, English physiologist, discusses a hypothetical situation in which some vinegar is put in contact with one of the sensitive end organs of taste on the tongue. If the nerve fiber conducting the impulse provoked by the vinegar were to be cut and grafted onto a nerve fiber leading from the ear to the brain, nothing would be tasted. Instead, "you would hear a very loud and startling noise. Every time the nerve end in your tongue was stimulated, you would have a similar hallucination."[7] If an auditory nerve were "misconnected" with an optic nerve you would, when you heard music, see visions.

Walter believes that, as regards all the senses, the "quality" of a sensation depends upon the parts of the brain reached by the nerve impulses involved, whereas the "intensity" of the sensation is a function of the frequency of the impulses.[8]

All sensory experience, then, appears to be transmitted in electro-chemical forms. For example, both external waves and light waves assume the same form internally on the way to the cerebral cortex.

How these electro-chemical impulses become aural and visual imagery is a problem which remains for the neurologists, but for learning theory the implication is clear. The strength and consistency of a sensory input signal is the key to learning. The brain will form an image of any sensory impression which is strong and consistent and, as far as learning is concerned, the precise mode of the sensory exposure, visual, auditory, etc., is secondary. The brain can learn through any of these major sensory systems. The case of Helen Keller[9] is well known and strikingly illustrative of the capacity of the central nervous system to function effectively with a minimum of sensory data. Despite the fact that for most of her life she lacked visual and auditory experience, this remarkable woman became in many respects a superior human being.

The human aptitude for language learning, then, does not depend upon any one sensory modality. There is every reason to believe that if we set up conditions for visual language which would parallel those we already have for aural language, the brain would master visual symbols just as readily as it does aural symbols. This means that the child would begin to understand written words just as naturally and rapidly as he does spoken words. Gates, a pioneer in reading theory who studied the perceptual process in reading, indicated that as far as he was aware, "there is no evidence that printed words are more difficult to perceive or distinquish than spoken words."[10]

Charles C. Fries, Professor Emeritus of the University of Michigan, has also spoken to this point:

> The process of receiving a message through "talk" is a responding to the language signals of his native language code—language signals that make their contact with his nervous system by sound vibrations through the ear. The process of getting the same message (the same meanings) by "reading" is a responding to the same set of language signals that make their contact with his nervous system by light vibrations through the eye. The message is the same; the language code is the same; the language signals are the same for both "talking" and "reading." The only essential difference here is the fact that in "talk" the means of connection to the human nervous system consists of patterns of sound waves stimulating nerves in the eye.[11]

Let us now take a closer look at the nature of the language process. Language is in essence a system of communication, and in this basic sense men share language with many other life forms. What makes human language unique is its great complexity, abstractness and range of application. Language is man's greatest invention and the single characteristic that most clearly differentiates him from his biological competitors.[12]

Language exists in several forms and may be communicated through any one of the three major sensory systems: visual, auditory or tactile. Although we normally tend to limit language to the visual and auditory channels, it is important to appreciate that man can also process symbols through the sense of touch. Touch reading has usually been limited to braille for the blind, but there is some research today which is exploring the uses of touch language in other situations.[18] But whatever the form, the characteristics which distinguish human language from animal language is the uniquely human ability to think about and discuss things and actions in their absence. This is accomplished by a system of symbols which we call words. Certain sounds or written marks are taken to stand for objects, their actions and relationships, and these symbols become then a code by which we can send and receive messages to and from one another.

It is important to note two things in connection with this process. First, the code as such does not constitute the concepts or ideas which are to be communicated. The word for "man" differs in each language, but the concept is essentially the same. The form of the words "hombre" and "man" have little in common, yet they both stand for the same idea. The sounds and written marks are only meaningful when they are interpreted by a human brain which has mastered the code being used. Words are not ideas, as such, but a necessary means through which ideas can be elaborated and communicated. Human language is not primarily the ability to make sounds or marks, but rather, it is the invention of symbols to express concepts. Communication is the expression and interpretation of symbols whether they be written or spoken—whether in Spanish, English, or some other language.

As this communication is a two-way street, language can be classified as either expressive or receptive. These categories can in turn be further analyzed. In expressive language we have, first, the idea to be communicated and, second, the code or symbol system selected to send the message—for example Spanish or English; and last, the mechanical form used to send the signals, such as sounds or written marks.

Reception can also be analyzed in a similar way. First, there is the signal received by the eye or ear; next, the translation of the physical code into a sensory message sent to the brain; and finally, the interpretation of the code.

Let us suppose that one person wishes to convey the idea of "table" to another. First, there must be some notion of "table" in the mind of the sender. Second, he must know a word form for "table" which the receiver will recognize. This word is a kind of code signal which could be a series of marks, a pattern of sounds, or perhaps a system of raised dots, as in braille. Third, the sender must emit or send the signals to the receiver.

At the other end of the channel, the receiver picks up the signal as a sensation and then rapidly organizes it into a perception or recognition of word form. Once the word form has been clearly perceived by the receiver who is familiar with the particular code system, he experiences his own, parallel idea of "table."

There is a cycle in this process by which we go from concept in the mind of the sender, through sensory impressions, to concept in the mind of the receiver. The sensory impressions, or images, function as "catalytic agents" which enter into the communication process as mechanisms to "trigger off" ideas and yet do not constitute the ideas as such. For example, in German, in order to convey the notion of "table," we must say or write the word "Tisch." In Spanish, the same idea is communicated by "mesa." In neither language does the pattern of sounds, as such, nor the visual configuration, as such, suggest a table.

There is nothing in the word "table" which relates it to real tables. As a matter of fact, although English is originally a Germanic language, our word "table" is French in origin. We use a French word today because the Norman French won the battle of Hastings in 1066 and changed the course of the development of modern English. Had they lost, we would probably be using an Anglo-Saxon word.

What we have in the symbolic process is a system of arbitrary sounds and marks which serve to trigger off ideas which men share in common. But for our purposes it is important to note that in any form of communication, written or spoken, there must be at one point a clearly perceived sensory signal functioning as a word. However familiar one might be with tables as objects, if the word form being used to convey the idea were not clearly perceived, there would be no communication.

The word is a symbol which men have agreed will stand for their experience of things. Words are a code in visual, auditory, or tactile form, a kind of system of dots and dashes which men use to communicate ideas. Unless both parties know the code, communication breaks down.

A few aspects of human language reception are worth special note. The human senses are called receptors; and there are several, but chiefly, as far as language is concerned, they are the ears, eyes, and organs of touch. These sensory faculties convey coded sensory data to the brain, but they do not analyze the message content. Moreover, as we have noted, they do not transmit the actual sound or light waves as these forces impinge upon the retina or tympanic membrane. All sensory receptors transduct external forces into an electro-chemical current which is sent through the pathways of the nervous system to the brain. Let us point out again that it is the same kind of "current" that goes to the higher centers in the brain, whether it be via the auditory, optic or tactile nerves. Aural, visual, or tactile impressions are all alike in this respect. To the brain they are patterns of neural impulses of an electro-chemical nature. It is the brain which interprets these patterns and makes them meaningful.

The heart of the language process is the interpretation of neural patterns. It is not the code or external language form; nor can it be the senses through which the messages are received. Both the particular code and the sensory modality are incidental to the process. The cognitive faculties in the brain constitute the essence of the language process. Therefore, if the brain of the child is able to master language through one sensory modality, there is every reason to believe this brain could learn language through any of the major sensory systems.

SUMMARY

In this chapter, we have argued that any language aptitude possessed by the young child must be a function of the brain and not of any particular avenue of impression. In other words, the ear does not hear nor does the eye see; it is the brain that operates these "modalities." Therefore, where conditions are comparable, any language learning possible through one major sensory channel must be possible through the other major sensory channels. Understanding spoken symbols and understanding printed ones is essentially the same in that both require a human intelligence. It is man's power to create abstract concepts that enables him to read and to understand spoken language forms.

REFERENCES

1. ANDERSON, IRVING H., and DEARBORN, WALTER F.: *The Psychology of Teaching Reading.* New York, Ronald Press, 1952, p. 72.
2. GATES, ARTHUR, et al.: Unsolved problems in reading: a symposium. *Elementary English,* Oct., 1954, pp. 325-338.
3. HERMANN, KNUD: *Reading Disability: A Medical Study of Word-Blindness and Related Handicaps.* Springfield, Thomas, 1959, p. 33.
4. MOWER, O. HOBART: *Learning Theory and Personality Dynamics.* New York, Ronald Press, 1950, pp. 688-726.
5. WARREN, HOWARD: *Dictionary of Psychology.* Boston, Houghton Mifflin, 1934, p. 270.
6. LANGFELD, H.S.: Note on a case of chromaesthesia. *Psychological Bulletin, 11*:113-114, 1914.
7. WALTER, W. GREY: *The Living Brain.* New York, Norton, 1953, pp. 73-74.
8. *Ibid.,* p. 74.
9. ALLUISI, EARL: Toward optimizing man's tactile communication. *Perceptual and Motor Skills, 12*:235-245, 1961.
10. GATES, ARTHUR, et al.: *Op. cit.* p. 334.
11. FRIES, CHARLES: *Linguistics and Reading.* New York, Holt, Rinehart and Winston, 1962, p. 119.
12. ANDERSON, JOHN: Child development and the growth process. *The Thirty-Eighth Yearbook of the National Society for the Study of Education: Part 1, Child Development and the Curriculum,* Edited by G. Whipple. Bloomington, Ill., Public School Publishing Co., 1939, p. 32.
13. HIRSCH, JOSEPH: Tactile reading. *Claremont College Reading Conference: Twenty-Second Yearbook,* 1957, Claremont, California, Claremont College, 1957, pp. 41-47.

Chapter Four

EARLY READING RECONSIDERED

MAIN POINTS

Children's early exposure to printed symbols traditionally limited and inadequate.
Child-learner's brain needs time to establish perceptual patterns.
Child's need for exposure to auditory symbols taken for granted.
Our "unconscious" assumption that preschoolers cannot learn to read.
Contrast in conditions for learning speech at home and reading in school.
Montessori's success in teaching children to read before six.
Historical reports of parents who taught preschoolers to read.
Experimental evidence for teaching reading before six favorable.
Overall success of past and present early reading programs.
Potential of television in teaching reading.

IN THE PREVIOUS CHAPTER, the point was made that learning to process language symbols as neural patterns is a unitary process. Learning speech and learning print, it was noted, are two basically equivalent aspects of man's underlying language capacity. If the brain of the child can master language regardless of the code or sensory modality involved—if understanding spoken symbols and understanding printed symbols are essentially the same—then why does the child not acquire reading as easily as he acquires speech? Why are we not surrounded by early readers?

The answer to these questions is quite simple. Children are not given adequate exposure to the visual symbols of reading. Very few children are ever given any opportunity to learn the perceptual forms of written language. Because we have always assumed that speech must precede reading, very few educators have given any serious consideration to teaching very young children to read. An exception to this is B. F. Skinner,[1] a contemporary proponent of programmed instruction and teaching machines, who has in his writings come to stress the importance of early exposure to symbolic forms and the role of reinforcement in the learning process. He has even discussed the value of exposure to symbols through teaching machines in nursery school. But the general practice of our society is to limit the child's language to speech. While parents automatically expose their children daily to spoken language, there are no domestic or social practices which would as a matter of course expose the child to visual language forms. The printed word reaching most children does not meet the criterion of adequate exposure, while sounds are addressed to the child as commands and encouragements which, when associated with particular situations, become in the mind of the child a sign and eventually, a symbol of the action desired.[2] In fact, there is so much "talking" in a normal home environment that children learn the significance of words without much formal effort on the part of the parents.

With visual symbols the situation is quite the reverse. In our society, there is no special recognition of the child's learning capacity. His ability to master speech is "taken for granted" and consequently not understood. We unconsciously assume that children will learn to talk just as we unconsciously assume that *they cannot learn to read*. Therefore, we have evolved no cultural practices which would give the child extensive exposure to printed symbols. We make no effort to provide for the child a visual, symbolic experience comparable to his aural experience.

Whereas the child's world of objects and actions is labeled with symbolic sounds, it has not been customary to label his world with the corresponding visual symbols. In the experience of children, everything has a "spoken tag." These tags are constantly repeated by parents, older siblings, and other adults. Children are bombarded with sound-symbols from their first few months of life, but they are not given a parallel visual experience. Therefore, whether or not very young children have an aptitude for early reading, in present practice they have little opportunity to employ it.

Arthur and Carolyn Staats, of Arizona State University, have been investigating reading from a behavioristic point of view. They

EARLY READING RECONSIDERED

have observed that the stimuli involved in learning to read are no more complex than those involved in learning to speak. Why, then, they ask, should speech be mastered so easily and universally, and reading be more difficult and less successful?

They offer the following explanation:

> Speech is acquired in a functional manner with immediate reinforcement, over a long period of time, while reading is taught in a concentrated period of time to a large group with little guarantee of adequate reinforcement.[3]
>
> [In fact, they suggest that the learning environment in school is so unfavorable for some children that it produces an aversive response. These children learn to avoid the reading situation.]

In the case of visual language development, then, none of the conditions for learning are normally met in the child's environment. The visual symbols of our language are presented in a form which suits the convenience of the printer. Packed together, in relatively small size, with no clear referents, printed words give the child little opportunity to become familiar with their meaning.

Unlike spoken words, which are directed at the child's ear slowly and clearly, printed words are usually so small that even adults with fading visual powers have trouble reading them and need lenses to correct their presbyopia. Obviously, the average child does not get a clear visual signal from the printed page and would have great difficulty learning to recognize words under the present circumstances. By making the words so small we are, in a sense, keeping reading a secret from children. One psychological study of typography, for example, indicates that 24-point type face size may be desirable for children under seven years of age.[4] The child has amazing power to master language, but it can only be stimulated by a clear strong input.

The second condition, repetition, is not met either. This, too, is a consequence of our method of printing in small type. The few large captions in books and on objects such as cereal boxes to which children are repeatedly exposed are, in fact, learned by most normal children, to the surprise of their parents. Most children learn at least a few of the signs, symbols, words, and slogans which appear frequently in their environment. But we "unconsciously" keep them away from any consistent exposure to the great majority of printed words.

The third condition, meaningfulness, is also unfulfilled, for even if the size of type were larger, the problem would not be completely solved because of the general format of the printed page. In a page of print we crowd the words together, and except for occasional captions, there is no way for the child to establish a connection between the word and the object. Again, with aural language the opposite is true. We address the child directly and point and gesture to objects and, in a clear voice, name them. In being exposed to aural language the child has every opportunity to see the relationship between the spoken word and the object named. On a printed page there is little possibility of his making such a connection.

Whatever secondary factors may be involved, the main reason why children do not master visual symbols is that none of the conditions for learning are presently fulfilled in their environment. The format of the page is such that the printed words do not physically match any object or action, and therefore, to the learner are largely meaningless. Moreover, because most parents have always assumed that children could not learn to read, they have made no effort to explain the "mysteries" of printed language to the child. The language aptitude of the child does not enable him to learn to read when society gives him no opportunity to employ it.

Although it has not been usual for parents to attempt to teach babies to read, there have been a considerable number of inquisitive and imaginative people who have taught very young children to read. Perhaps the most impressive demonstration of teaching reading to the very young was accomplished by Doctor Maria Montessori. Doctor Montessori, the pioneer Italian physician-educator, proved conclusively some sixty years ago that children of five could learn to read under proper circumstances.[5] From that time until now, a few schools modelled on her principles have been teaching young children to read in different countries throughout the world. Unfortunately, until very recently the full implications of her work were not appreciated by most educators.

However, reading in the preschool child has now become a popular scientific subject, and new attention is being paid to the work of Doctor Montessori. In the United States since the mid-1950's, there has been a rebirth of interest in the Montessori methodology, and there are now more than 200 schools employing the Montessori approach to early childhood education in this country.

Mrs. Nancy Rambusch, founder of the American Montessori Society and the Whitby School—the first of the new wave of Montessori schools—has described the implications of the Montessori method for American public education in a book called *Learning How to Learn*.[6] The Montessori movement is spreading throughout the United States, and everywhere the success of the method is proving the "readiness" of the pre-school child for reading training.

In 1918, Lewis Terman, famous for his studies of gifted children, reported a case of early reading in which the early experience appears to have created a gifted child. This particular child had been making normal progress until her father, a lawyer with no formal background in educational theory, taught her to read. Subsequently she was classified as gifted and made an excellent school record. Terman followed her academic career with much interest, and the favorable results of her early intellectual stimulation have been recorded.[7]

Another very similar case is reported in the book *Natural Education*[8] by Winifred Stoner. This remarkable woman set out to make her child superior through early intellectual stimulation. She believed that every human being was potentially unique and creative, but that a dull unstimulating environment in childhood inhibited the development of intellectual powers. She had only her own daughter to work with, but the results she obtained were amazing. One case is not enough to satisfy scientific standards of proof, but insomuch as she predicted in advance what her efforts would accomplish and then accomplished it, her book deserves more attention than it has received. One of the central accomplishments of her little girl was early reading.

William Fowler, of Yale University, has reported an unpublished study made by Muriel Brown in 1924.[9] Brown, using flash cards, posters, and a primer trained a group of pre-school children to read. Fowler notes particularly the records of Roger, a very bright

(140 IQ) three-year-old boy and Catherine, a below average (91 IQ) three-year-old girl. The children were given only twenty minutes of training per day, five days per week for three months. Yet Fowler reports that even Catherine, in thirty-six lessons, learned to read eleven pages of her primer, while Roger reached the same point in twenty-six lessons. Both children could read their charts, and the recombination of words upon the charts with perfect ease.

Omar K. Moore, also of Yale, has been experimenting with a group of children as young as three years of age.[10] By giving the children individual attention and special materials appropriate to their level of perception, Moore has succeeded in teaching these children to read.

These foregoing efforts are of great importance in demonstrating the reading aptitude of the young child, but the evidence is by no means limited to these examples. In reviewing the cases of early reading that have come to light from historical sources, it is most impressive to note that a variety of methods of early reading instruction have been successful.

Children repeatedly exposed to visual symbols that are large enough to see, and that are clearly and repeatedly associated with some object, have learned to read the symbols. Television has given the observant parent first-hand experience with this fact. It has become commonplace to hear parents comment on the fact that their very young children recognize commercial names and symbols that have appeared (all too frequently, perhaps) on television programs. In fact, one study reports the case of a young boy whose initial reading vocabulary included a whiskey brand name.[11] If such a term is not an educational ideal, then let us hasten to emulate the Madison Avenue psychologists who have for some years recognized a basic law of learning: present large, clear, meaningful stimuli, and repeat them! If we want children to start their reading experience with something other than TV commercial slogans, then we would do well to imitate the format and repetition of advertising.

If we consider the nature of the language aptitude manifest in the child's mastery of speech, there is every reason to believe that similar exposure to visual symbols would result in the child's learning to read at a very young age. If from the first year the child were surrounded with visual symbols meaningfully related to objects in the child's world, he would come to read these just as he comes to understand the spoken symbols. Parents could, with perhaps somewhat greater effort than they devote at present to story-telling, expose children to printed language.[12]

Of course, speech is the dominant mode of communication in our society, and there is every reason to believe that it will remain so. There are good reasons why man learned to talk before he began reading and writing. Speech is more convenient and more personal. The historical dominance of oral language leads us to expect that this dominance will appear in the language development of the normal child. It seems probable that spoken language will always precede visual language and will to some extent dominate the language process in the child. But there is no reason why visual language development could not also get a start early in the child's life. Moreover, it seems likely that this visual language would reinforce the child's spoken language development. Visual and oral symbols would become closely matched in the child's memory. All through his formative years, day after day, these labels and word pictures would surround the child just as at present he is surrounded by spoken language.

In the beginning, some organized efforts will be required from the adult world to call the child's attention to the relatively uninteresting visual symbols. Parents will need the assistance of psychologists and educators in devising games and techniques which will encourage the child to become interested in, to recognize, and to remember the visual words. There is no question that television could perform a great service here. Children's shows could informally introduce children to many basic, simple words. If a few minutes of the hours children spend watching television involved some sight recognition exercises, perhaps in the form of games, most children could master dozens of words painlessly. Moreover, the nursery schools and kindergartens, which at present tend often to be babysitting operations rather than educational institutions, could continue the process started in the home.

It is important to note that none of the procedure suggested above involves any formal presentation or organized instruction such as the normal child encounters in the first grade. All that should be required is an informal exposure to large printed words throughout the preschool period. It need not be a matter of making the very young child an independent reader, so much as exposing his formative brain to visual language. Name cards, pictures with large labels, story books with fewer words in large type—all can help do the job well.

Nor would it be essential that children have a complete grasp of all the conceptual implications of the words mastered, but only that they build up familiarity with the basic forms of visual language. The more complex aspects of reading: phonetic analysis, advanced vocabulary development, spelling, and grammar could wait until the child entered school. In school, the child's visual language development could be accelerated more formally just as now his spoken language is expanded.

Let us recall that by age five the average child, with no formal effort, has developed a vocabulary of several thousand words which he can express in all of the syntactical forms of adult speech. The five-year-old can understand complex actions and can narrate coherently his own experiences. There is no reason why this same power should be limited to his ear. Why not provide the same conditions of exposure which would permit the child's brain to learn to read just as he learns to talk? Why could not the brain of the five-year-old be able to use visual symbols just as fluently as he uses spoken words? The child should be able to read about any idea he can discuss.

Children have not learned to read because the mode by which society presents visual symbols to the child is not designed for the child. Moreover, the occasional efforts made by a few interested adults to teach young children to read tend to bear this out because they have been highly successful. Wherever children have been exposed to visual symbols that are large enough for them to see, as on television, and meaningfully associated with some object or action repeatedly, the children have learned to read.

Finally, we have pointed out, the child's language aptitude *decreases* with age, and the older a person becomes the more difficult will it be for him to master language. Therefore, we must infer that the longer reading experience is delayed, the more difficult will be its mastery. Indeed as the next chapter will discuss, the extent and seriousness of the "reading problems" in our society, when contrasted with the lesser incidence of "speech problems" in the same culture, suggests strongly that something is amiss in the way we teach children to read.

SUMMARY

Our society has not institutionalized the provision of a "prepared environment" for all preschoolers which would give them the opportunity for systematic experience leading to the learning of printed symbols. If very young children have the capacity for learning printed symbols when properly presented (as they do with spoken symbols) this capacity will not likely find expression in their present surroundings, where early reading may even be actively discouraged. Extensively exposed as they are to speech but not to printed symbols, it is certainly not surprising to find that preschoolers generally learn to master speech but not to read. Reading has not yet been put on the preschooler's informal agenda.

Doctor Maria Montessori was one of the first persons to recognize the importance of fully utilizing the young child's "sensitive period" for language learning. She deliberately exposed the young learner to an environment containing an array of programmed materials with which he could learn to read and write—largely by teaching himself. Speaking of the results of her experiments in matching the environment to the young learner's needs, she says:

> In any case, almost all of the normal children treated with our method begin to write at four years, and at five know how to read and write, at least as well as children who have finished the first elementary. They could enter the second elementary a year in advance of the time when they are admitted to first.[13]

A number of other investigators have reported their success in teaching young children to read, although no single method employed can as yet be specified "best." We may expect that research will continue to develop and refine the methodology of teaching early reading.

REFERENCES

1. SKINNER, B.F.: *Cumulative Record.* Enlarged Ed., New York, Appleton-Century-Crofts, 1961, pp. 143-182.
2. HOLMES, JACK A.: The brain and the reading process. *Claremont*

College Reading Conference: Twenty-Second Yearbook, 1957, Claremont, California, Claremont College, 1957, p. 59.
3. STAATS, ARTHUR, and STAATS, CAROLYN: A comparison of the development of speech and reading behavior with implications for research. *Child Development,* 33:831-846, 1962.
4. BURT, CYRIL, et al.: A psychological study of typography. *British Journal of Statistical Psychology,* 8:29-57, 1955.
See also, Doman, Glenn: *How to Teach Your Baby to Read.* New York, Random House, 1964.
5. OREM, R.C.: (Ed.), *A Montessori Handbook.* New York, Putnam, 1965. Capricorn edition, 1966.
6. RAMBUSCH, NANCY: *Learning How to Learn: An American Approach To Montessori.* Baltimore, Helicon Press, 1962.
7. TERMAN, LEWIS: An experiment in infant education. *The Journal of Applied Psychology,* 1918.
8. STONER, WINIFRED: *Natural Education,* Indianapolis, Bobbs-Merrill, 1914.
9. FOWLER, WILLIAM: Cognitive learning in infancy and early childhood. *Psychological Bulletin,* 59:131, 1962.
10. MOORE, OMAR: *Autotelic Responsive Environments and Exceptional Children.* Hamden, Conn., Responsive Environments, Inc., 1963.
11. CARROLL, HERBERT: *A Genius in the Making.* New York, McGraw-Hill, 1940.
12. See Appendix.
13. MONTESSORI, MARIA: *The Montessori Method.* New York, Stokes, 1912, pp. 302-303.

SUGGESTED READINGS, BRIEFLY ANNOTATED

1. ANDERSSON, T.: The optimum age for beginning the study of modern language. *International Review of Education,* 6: 298-306, 1960.

According to the author, the optimum age for beginning the study of modern languages is between four and eight.

2. BRUNER, J.: *The Process of Education.* Cambridge, Harvard University Press, 1960.

Jerome S. Bruner is the Director of the Center for Cognitive Studies at Harvard. This small but highly influential book is his report on an educational conference held in September 1959, when some thirty-five scientists, scholars, and educators met to discuss how education in science might be improved in our primary and secondary schools. The ten days of meetings considered learning theory, motivation, curriculum, readiness, and teaching aids. In general, Bruner favors an earlier start in many subjects and a greater stress on "structure rather than detail."

Ideas should be taught by challenging the student to think hypothetically, not in formulae.

    3. DURKIN, D.: Should the very young be taught to read? *National Educational Association Journal*, 52:23-26, 1963.

Kindergarten children should have the opportunity to begin to learn to read. Ways to identify children who are ready to begin learning to read and suggestions for teaching them to read are given.

    4. HUNT, J. McV.: *Intelligence and Experience*, New York, Ronald Press, 1961.

This is an extensive review of the literature in psychology which examines the role of early environmental stimulation as a determinant in adult intelligence.

Hunt questions the normative schedules of the Gesell school, which are largely based upon an assumption of predetermined development.

    5. MACPHEE, H.: Percepts and images as primary factors in thinking. *Proceedings of the 40th Annual Education Conference*, Newark, Delaware, School of Education, University of Delaware, 1958, pp. 79-82.

"Another fact about imagery is of special interest to those who work with young children. And this is the discovery that children have more vivid imagery than adults, but that with increasing age, the vividness of imagery becomes dulled."

    6. PIAGET, J.: *The Language and Thought of the Child*. 2nd Ed. London, Routledge & Kegan Paul, 1948, 246.

The study of the development and function of the child's language, and how he thinks, with extensive treatment of the child's questions.

For a very helpful analysis of Piaget's work, and that of his colleague Inhelder, see *Intelligence and Experience*, by J. McV. Hunt, above.

    7. PINCUS, M., and MORGENSTERN, F.: Should children be taught to read earlier? *The Reading Teacher*, 18:37-42, 1964.

"Perhaps much of the difficulty and some of the controversy that arises in considering the question 'Should younger children be taught to read?' could be avoided by asking, instead, more specific questions, such as: 'Which characteristics enable children to learn to read successfully before they enter the first grade?' 'How can we best help children who are already reading?' 'Which methods and materials are most effective for introducing young children to reading?' In fact, can we justify not asking such questions?" p. 42.

    8. STEIN, M., and HEINZE, S.: *Creativity and the Individual: Summaries of Selected Literature in Psychology and Psychiatry*. A publication of the University of Chicago Graduate School of Business. Glencoe, Ill., Free Press, 1960.

Contains a detailed annotated bibliography on many aspects of creativity, such as "Early Experiences" and "Cognitive Factors."
    9. TAYLOR, C.W.: *The Second (1957) University of Utah Conference on the Identification of Creative Scientific Talent.* Salt Lake City, University of Utah Press, 1958.

See especially such selections as B. S. Bloom's "Some effects of cultural, social, and educational conditions on creativity."
    10. VYGOTSKY, L.: *Thought and Language.* Edited and transslated by E. Hanfmann and G. Vakar, New York, Wiley, 1962.

The author was interested in, among other things, the possibility of stimulating a more rapid development of thought processes.
    11. WITTY, PAUL: Two studies of children's interest in TV. *Elementary English,* 251-57, 1952.

The "average" five-year-old watches TV for twenty-one hours weekly.
    12. WOLFF, W.: *The Personality of the Preschool Child.* New York, Grune & Stratton, 1947.

Compares the child's mind and world with those of the adult and indicates the need for adult appreciation of the basic differences. Wolff sees much untapped learning potential in the very young child.

ADDITIONAL READINGS

1. AMMONS, R.: Experiential factors in visual form perception: I. review and formulation of problems. *The Journal of Genetic Psychology,* 84:3-25, 1954.
2. BEVAN, WILLIAM: Perception: evolution of a concept. *Psychological Review,* 65:34-55, 1958.
3. BRUNER, J., MILLER, G., and ZIMMERMAN, C.: Discriminative skill and discriminative matching in perceptual recognition. *Journal of Experimental Psychology,* 49:187-192, 1955.
4. CANTOR, J.: Amount of pretraining as a factor in stimulus predifferentiation and performance set. *Journal of Experimental Psychology,* 50:180-184, 1955.
5. DREVER, J.: Perceptual learning. *Annual Review of Psychology.* Palo Alto, Annual Reviews, Inc., 1960.
6. GATES, A., and BOND, G.: Reading readiness: a study of factors determining success and failure in beginning reading. *Teachers College Record,* 37:679-685, 1936.
7. GIBSON, J., and GIBSON, E.: Perceptual learnings: differentiation or enrichment? *Psychological Review,* 62:32-41, 1955.
8. HARLOW, H.: The Formation of Learning Sets. Paper presented as the presidential address of the Midwestern Psychological Association meetings in St. Paul, May 7, 1948.

9. HARLOW, H., and WARREN, J.: Formation and transfer of discrimination learning sets. *Journal of Comparative and Physiological Psychology, 45*:482-489, 1952.
10. JOHNSON, M.: Factors related to disability in reading. *Journal of Experimental Education, 26*:1-26, 1957.
11. MYERS, G.: Reading to babies and young children. *Education. 77*:576-579, 1957.
12. NOLAN, C.: Readability of large types: a study of type sizes and type styles. *International Journal for the Education of the Blind, 9*:41-44, 1959.
13. PIAGET, J.: *The Child's Conception of the World.* Paterson, New Jersey, Littlefield, Adams, 1960.
14. RAZRAN, G.: Conditioning and perception. *Psychological Review. 62*: 83-192, 1955.
15. RIOPELLE, A.: Learning sets from minimum stimuli. *Journal of Experimental Psychology, 49*:28-32, 1955.
16. SOLLEY, C. and SANTOS, J.: Perceptual learning with partial verbal reinforcement. *Perceptual and Motor Skills, 8*:183-193, 1958.
17. STEVENSON, H., and MCBEE, G.: The learning of object and pattern discrimination by children. *Journal of Comparative and Physiological Psychology, 51*:752-754, 1958.
18. ZUCKERMAN, C., and ROCK, I.: A reappraisal of the roles of past experience and innate organizing processes in visual perception. *Psychological Bulletin, 54*:269-296, 1957.

Chapter Five

TOWARD A THEORY OF READING DISABILITY

MAIN POINTS

Reading failures in our schools a serious national problem.
Most adults are reading problems to some extent.
Four types of reading problems:
1. physical;
2. psychological;
3. environmental;
4. functional.

Intelligence not the determining factor in majority of reading problems.
Importance of perceptual difficulties in functional reading problems.
Mastery of auditory imagery by functional reading problems.

THERE EXISTS IN OUR SOCIETY a puzzling incongruity between the general skill and effectiveness with which people use spoken language and their relatively ineffectual mastery of printed language. This is most clearly seen with children, for while, by and large, they have no difficulty learning to speak, many have serious difficulty learning to read, and few find reading mastery easy.

The authors recall in this connection the case of a boy who spent his first three years in Germany with his American parents. During those early formative years he learned to speak English fluently and had mastered enough German to behave bilingually, when his family returned to the United States. At the age of six, he started school and at the end of the first year was adjudged a reading problem, although his intelligence level was "average." Here we have a perplexing problem for the learning theorist. How is it that a preschooler of only average intelligence can learn informally to speak one or more languages but after a year of schooling be unable to read one language?

His difficulty was certainly not unique; a disturbingly high percentage of normal children have great difficulty learning to read. Doctor E. A. Betts, a leading figure in reading education, has indicated that from 25 to 35 per cent of first grade children, on a national average, fail to be promoted. Doctor Betts further notes: "By and large, promotion in this grade has been based upon reading ability."[1] In other words, nearly one child out of every three on the average fails to pass the first grade because of reading problems! Arthur Gates made similar observations in a book dealing with reading problems. He found that 99 per cent of first grade failures were due to reading, 90 per cent in grade two and by grade three 70 per cent. Gates wrote:

> Although it is not now universally agreed in school circles that pupils should not be promoted from the primary grades until they can read intelligently, the problem of dealing with retarded readers, even those of superior intelligence, is a serious one. No other subject presents such difficulties to the primary teacher.[2]

As the Gates figures indicate, the problem is not solved by the passage of time or the eventual "social" promotion of these problem readers. The reading specialists and educational theorists who have dominated the reading teaching field for the past thirty years have discussed the gravity of the situation. Paul Witty, a leading authority on methods of reading teaching, estimated that as many as one-third of our high school students are reading below an eighth grade level.[3]

The late William S. Gray, professor of reading and education at the University of Chicago for many years and author of a widely used series of basal readers, has written:

> Records of the achievement of pupils show that from 20 to 30 percent of the pupils who enter either the junior or senior high school read so poorly that they can engage in required reading only with great difficulty. Indeed, some of them are so much retarded in reading that it is impossible for them to read the books ordinarily used at their respective grade levels.[4]

Doctor James Bryant Conant commented in an article in the *Ladies Home Journal* that he had been in high schools where 30 per cent of the students were below the sixth grade level in reading achievement.[5]

Other evaluations of the problem have been even more grave. In a 1961 publication of the Council for Basic Education, it was estimated that 75 per cent of the school population are reading markedly below grade levels.[6] The fantastically high percentage of defective readers in our regular schools has been the subject of much similar comment from other interested persons.[7,8]

Nor is the problem limited to the school child, for most adults are much more comfortable with spoken language than with visual language. William S. Gray estimated that about one-half of the adult readers in America are unable to read well enough to keep abreast of current social and political issues. In several studies, Gray found most adults reading at a ninth grade level.[9]

By way of contrast, these same adults are quite capable of following spoken directions and giving expression to very complex verbal relationships.

It is not unusual in the authors' experience to find an individual who could not complete high school, because he read so poorly, capable of discussing baseball or some other sport in great depth. Such an individual, although he may have failed "world history," can relate the history of baseball in complex and logical sentences. His grasp of facts may be excellent and his word choice appropriate. His speech may even, on occasion, become imaginative and original. Obviously, he has a good mastery of both receptive and expressive speech. Why should this brain, that functions so naturally with the auditory imagery of spoken language, stumble and hesitate over the visual imagery of graphic language?

To answer this question, we must first look at the factors which inhibit reading in the school child and the adult. For the purposes of our discussion, individuals classified as reading problems can be grouped into four overlapping categories.

(1) There are the *physical* reading problems whose difficulty stems from one or more constitutional deficiencies, which in some cases may be genetically determined as with the Mongolian idiot, or be the result of injury, disease, or defective development. Individuals in this category have something wrong with their

organism—often the nervous system—which interferes with their mental development and learning.

(2) There are the *psychological* reading problems whose emotional disturbance is severe enough to block their learning capabilities.

(3) There are the *environmental* reading problems, who, because they have been exposed to harsh, unstimulating, or deprived conditions in home, school, or community have failed to develop necessary language skills and attitudes for reading. They have experienced educational and sociological deficits.

(4) There are the *functional* reading problems, who, while constituting the vast majority of reading problems, are yet in other respects essentially normal.

Conant, in speaking of those pupils who comprise the lower one-third in reading achievement noted in *Harpers*:

> The pupils who compose this lower one-third are not to be confused with the mentally backward (a far smaller group comprising only about five percent of a school or less). The great majority of them are normal, wholesome, even talented, responsible youth.[10]

From existing research there is no evidence that we can look to genetics or physical pathology to explain the millions of reading problems in our schools. In fact, one researcher commented that 80 per cent of the reading problems investigated had average or above average intelligence as measured on IQ tests.[11] The great majority have a good mastery of speech, and though a few may stutter, almost none have any difficulty understanding speech. Many of these reading problems have very high IQ's and manage to make successful careers for themselves in fields where they can compensate for their reading disability.[12]

Throughout the country there are hundreds of reading clinics where thousands of reading teachers provide remedial instruction for severe reading problems, and in the schools themselves there are many more "marginal" reading problems. These students read below their grade level and require special tutoring. And finally, even many successful students who can read well enough to make good grades in school do so only with great effort. In fact, there is only a small minority of students and adults who read rapidly and accurately with efficiency and ease.

In the category of functional reading problems we have individuals ranging from the high IQ non-reader in the clinic to the honor student reading at a painfully slow rate of speed.

There is no evidence of organic limitations blocking their reading development, and their other language skills are average or above. It is only in the perception of visual symbols that they function below normal levels.

The great majority of reading problems are able to function verbally. Many, if given oral tests, will score above the average in reasoning power, and they can handle the language abstraction of normal speech. In fact, many of these poor readers become expert listeners, mastering subject matter through discussion and lecture. In general, their intelligence seems higher than their reading performance indicates. But from the non-reader to the slow reader there is a characteristic area of difficulty, which is perceptual-associative in nature.

Functional reading problems, then, are not intellectual or cognitional problems. These people with reading limitations do not have a comprehension problem, for there is no question that they are able to process symbols with accuracy and speed *so long as these symbols are presented aurally.* It is only in the perception of visual symbols that they have difficulty. When these readers are confronted with the printed word, several related interferences arise. First, and most serious, the reader may block and simply get no recognition of the word at all. (It is important to note here, that it is perception or recognition of the *word form* that blocks the reader[13] and not cognition, as such, since if we give him the same word aurally, he may understand the word perfectly.) Second, they may reverse the words or they may reverse the letters so that "was" becomes "saw" or "d" becomes "b." This reversal tendency has been called strephosymbolia (twisted symbol), by Doctor Samuel Orton, a reading authority who developed a neurological theory of reading disability.[14] Third, they may misread words which are somewhat alike in configuration so that "horse" might be read for "house" or "same" for "some." Fourth, many have to sound out each word subvocally with throat and lip movements or "hear" the words mentally before they get any comprehension of the words. In this last instance, it would appear that the visual input of the word image is not adequate to trigger off meaning, and therefore the visual image must be reinforced with an auditory association before the brain integrates or comprehends.

It is most important to note that all of these factors which characterize reading problems, from the remedial to the developmental, are basically perceptual in nature:

1. *Blocking*: looking at words with no recognition.
2. *Reversals*: twisting words around so that "on," for example, becomes "no."
3. *Misreading*: reading one word for another, as "there" for "these" or "horse" for "house."
4. *Subvocalization*: marked dependence upon the reinforcement of the reading process with mechanics of speech. This factor ranges from gross movement of speech musculature to sounding or hearing mentally the words being read.

All of the above involve some difficulty with the act of recognition of words. The reader who mistakes "horse" for "house" is not confused conceptually. He would never mistake a horse for a house, nor would he confuse the spoken word "horse" for "house." Most of the printed words which the problem reader is unable to recognize represent concepts with which he is very familiar. There is some kind of defect in the problem reader's ability to discriminate and decode the visual forms of language, for the little black marks that constitute printed words twist about, change shape, or remain meaningless.

Tests designed to measure reading comprehension, when administered to these problem readers, actually measure their inability to recognize and associate the perceptual aspects of visual symbols as distinct from their semantic import. A close analogy would be a testing situation in which we attempted to measure verbal intelligence by giving a subject a test in a language with which he had only limited familiarity. Let us take, for example, a college student who has studied French for two years and administer an oral intelligence test. How significant would the results be? Yet, this is what happens to the defective reader in many reading comprehension tests. Both situations are parallel. In the first, the college student would do poorly because he was not fluent with the sound of French words. He would fail to see the solution to very easy problems only because he would be blocked by the unfamiliar word forms in the questions. So with the defective reader, for he also fails to solve simple problems only because he is blocked by a lack of fluency with the visual forms of language. When we attempt to test cognition in an area where the subject has perceptual limitations, all we measure are those limitations, not the underlying intelligence.

Reading problems in the functional category are not, then, comprehension problems, but perceptual problems. The functionally inadequate readers are unable to perceive the forms of visual symbols, and it is this that blocks their efforts to integrate these symbols into concepts. Once again, let us emphasize that the same concepts presented aurally will be readily comprehended.

SUMMARY

Because efficient reading is the most important skill required in the educative process, the poor reading performance of millions of children is a just cause for concern if not alarm. A majority of adults also read at levels far below standards necessary for full literacy.

In this chapter, four major types of reading problems were identified: physical, psychological, environmental, and functional. In turn, several factors, perceptual in nature, which the functional reading problems display were discussed. It was noted that functional reading problems are not impaired in intelligence or cognition. That is, they are able to comprehend verbal material which they can perceive adequately; they can "read" language when it is in the form of auditory imagery.

Available evidence strongly suggests that the majority of reading problems are not intellectual or cognitive in nature, but rather, perceptual in nature.

REFERENCES

1. BETTS, E.A.: *Foundations of Reading Instruction: With Emphasis on Differentiated Guidance.* New York, American Book Co., 1957. p. 29.

2. GATES, ARTHUR I.: *The Improvement of Reading: A Program of Diagnostic & Remedial Measures,* 3rd Ed., New York, Macmillan, 1951, pp. 2-3.
3. WITTY, PAUL A.: The Improvement of Reading Abilities. *55th Yearbook of the National Society for the Study of Education,* Chicago, University of Chicago Press, 1956, pp. 252-253.
4. GRAY, WILLIAM: The language arts—reading. *Implications of Research For the Classroom Teacher.* Washington, 1939, p. 138.
5. Cited by Walcutt, Charles, in *Tomorrow's Illiterates: The State of Reading Instruction Today.* Boston, Little, Brown, 1961.
6. WALCUTT, CHARLES: (Ed.) *Tomorrow's Illiterates: The State of Reading Instruction Today.* p. 11.
7. TERMAN, SIBYL, and WALCUTT, CHARLES: *Reading: Chaos and Cure.* New York, McGraw-Hill, 1958.
8. MCCRACKEN, GLENN: *The Right to Learn.* Chicago, Henry Regnery, 1959.
9. GRAY, WILLIAM: How Well Do Adults Read? Adult Reading. *55th Yearbook of the National Society for the Study of Education.* Chicago, University of Chicago Press, 1956.
10. Cited by Walcutt, Charles: (Ed.), *Tomorrow's Illiterates: The State of Reading Instruction Today.* p. 8.
11. AUSTIN, MARY C.: Identifying Readers Who Need Corrective Instruction. *Corrective Reading in Classroom and Clinic.* Robinson, Helen M., (Ed.), Chicago, University of Chicago Press, 1953, pp. 19-25.
12. TERMAN, SIBYL, and WALCUTT, CHARLES: *Op. cit.* pp. 20-25.
13. HOLMES, JACK: The brain and the reading process. *Claremont College Reading Conference: Twenty-Second Yearbook,* Claremont, Claremont College, 1957, p. 58.
14. ORTON, SAMUEL: *Reading, Writing, and Speech Problems in Children: A Presentation of Certain Types of Disorders in the Development of the Language Faculty.* New York, Norton, 1937.

SUGGESTED READINGS, BRIEFLY ANNOTATED

1. BUSWELL, G.: The relationship between perceptual and intellectual processes in reading. *California Journal of Educational Research,* 8:99-103, 1957.

The author believes that the "new" element to be mastered by the student in learning to read is the perceptual recognition of the printed verbal symbols.

2. COLEMAN, J.: Perceptual retardation in reading disability cases. *Journal of Educational Psychology,* 44:497-503, 1953.

Retardation in perceptual differentiation was found to be cumulative with age.

3. _____: Perceptual Retardation in Reading Disability. *Perceptual and Motor Skills, 9*:117, 1959.

Brief report of investigation into retardation in visual perceptual development as characteristic of reading disability cases.

4. CANTOR, G.: Effects of three types of pretraining on discrimination learning in preschool children. *Journal of Experimental Psychology, 49*:339-342, 1955.

The possession of names for the stimuli in a learning task enhanced performance on that task.

5. DURRELL, D.: *Improving Reading Instruction.* Yonkers-on-Hudson, New York, World Book, 1956.

See "Erroneous concepts of reading readiness," pp. 46-48. The author discusses the following false concepts: "mysterious appearance" concept, emotional and personality-adjustment concept, and mental-age concept.

6. GATES, A.: A study of the role of visual perception, intelligence, and certain associative processes in reading and spelling. *Journal of Educational Psychology, 17*:433-445 1926.

Word perception was the ability most closely associated with achievement in reading and spelling.

7. _____: Implications of the psychology of perception for word study. *Education, 75*:589-595.

Learning to see words is not unlike learning to see other things.

8. GIBSON, E.: Improvement in perceptual judgements as a function of controlled practice or training. *Psychological Bulletin,* November, 1953.

Review of literature on perception as learned.

9. KURTZ, K.: Discrimination of complex stimuli: the relationship of training and test stimuli in transfer of discrimination. *Journal of Experimental Psychology, 50*:283-292, 1955.

The findings are in close accord with those of an earlier study by Lashley involving learning of rats. Under appropriate conditions, positive transfer of discrimination was obtained.

10. MEEK, L.: *A Study of Learning and Retention in Young Children.* New York, Bureau of Publications, Teachers College, Columbia University, 1925.

The great importance of "initial perceptual reactions" in reading success.

11. MEYERS, C., and DINGMAN, H.: The structure of abilities at the preschool ages: Hypothesized Domains. *Psychological Bulletin, 57*:514-532, 1960.

See "Visual Perception," pp. 526-527.

12. NISSEN, H.: A study of performance tests given to a group of native African children. *British Journal of Psychology,* 25:308, 1935.

Nissen found that these children, perfectly normal in most respects, had great difficulty in perceiving geometrical shapes and designs. Nissen concluded that their perceptual limitations were a product of cultural "sets." Having never been exposed to these forms, the children found them difficult to "see." Nissen's findings add weight to the notion that the perception of shape is to some extent learned, and that an early exposure to letter and word shapes might aid in the mastery of written language.

13. POSTMAN, L., and ROSENZWEIG, M.: Perceptual recognition of words. *Journal of Speech and Hearing Disorders,* 22, 1957.

Speed and accuracy of word recognition depends on familiarity and practice.

14. RUSSELL, D.: *Children's Thinking.* Boston, Ginn, 1956. See Chapter 3, "Percepts," and "Teaching for the Improvement of Perceptual Abilities," pp. 349-352.
15. SPIKER, C.: Stimulus pretraining and subsequent performance in the delayed reaction experiment. *Journal of Experimental Psychology,* 52:107-111, 1956.

Subjects who learned names made more correct choices of the "baited" stimuli following delay than did subjects who had not learned names. This was particularly true of the younger subjects.

ADDITIONAL READINGS

1. ARNOULT, M.: Stimulus predifferentiation: some generalizations and hypotheses. *Psychological Bulletin,* 54:339-350, 1957.
2. BROADBENT, D.E.: *Perception and Communication.* New York, Pergamon Press, 1958.
3. BRUNNER, J., WALLACH, M., and GALANTER, E.: The identification of recurrent regularity. *The American Journal of Psychology,* 72: 200-209, 1959.
4. DODWELL, P.: Coding and learning in shape discrimination. *Psychological Review,* 68:373-382, 1961.
5. FREEDMAN, S., and HELD, R.: Sensory deprivation and perceptual lag. *Perceptual and Motor Skills,* 11:277-280, 1960.
6. GATES, A., and BOEKER, E.: A study of initial stages in reading by pre-school children. *Teachers College Record,* 24:469-488, 1923.
7. GOINS, J.: *Visual Perceptual Abilities and Early Reading Progress.* Chicago, University of Chicago Press, Supplementary Educational Monograph No. 87, 1958.
8. JOHANNSEN, D.: Black-white relation of figure and ground in nursery

school children's figure perception. *Perceptual and Motor Skills,* *10*:23-26, 1960.
9. KUENNE, M.: Experimental investigation of the relation of language to transposition behavior in young children. *Journal of Experimental Psychology, 36*:471-490, 1946.
10. MUEHL, S.: The effects of visual discrimination pretraining with word and letter stimuli on learning to read a word list in kindergarten children. *Journal of Educational Psychology, 52*:215-221, 1961.
11. O'NEIL, W.: Basic issues in perceptual theory. *Psychological Review, 65*:348-361, 1959.
12. POSTMAN, L.: Association theory and perceptual learning. *Psychological Review, 62*:438-446, 1955.
13. RAAB, S., DEUTSCH, M., and FREEDMAN, A.: Perceptual shifting and set in normal school children of different reading achievement levels. *Perceptual and Motor Skills, 10*:187-192, 1960.
14. ROBINSON, J.: The effect of learning verbal labels for stimuli on their later discrimination. *Journal of Experimental Psychology, 49*:112-115, 1955.
15. SMITH, G.: Visual perception: an event over time. *Psychological Review, 65*:306-313, 1957.
16. SPIKER, C.: Performance on a difficult discrimination following pretraining with distinctive stimuli. *Child Development, 30*:513-521, 1959.
17. VERNON, M.: The functions of schemata in perceiving. *Psychological Review, 62*:180-192, 1955.
18. YARCZOWER, M.: Conditioning test of stimulus-predifferentiation. *The American Journal of Psychology, 72*:572-577, 1959.

Chapter Six

SOME ORIGINS OF PERCEPTUAL DIFFICULTIES

MAIN POINTS

Origins of perceptual problems.
Importance of early exposure to auditory imagery for speech.
Early exposure to visual imagery equally important for reading.
Review of three stages in communication: sensory, perceptual, cognitive.
Role of experience in learning to see. Evidence from sensory deprivation in animals and the work of von Senden.
The brain as computer.
Importance of childhood sensitive period for establishing auditory and visual imagery of language.
Failure to establish sufficient visual imagery a major factor in functional reading problems.

THE ORIGINS OF THE PERCEPTUAL PROBLEMS discussed in the previous chapter lie in the nature of the brain's development. As has been suggested throughout this book, the brain appears to have an early period of sensitivity to sensory forms and, after that period is over, it becomes more and more difficult to imprint new forms on the matured brain. After the age of about six, most if not all human beings have begun to lose their language aptitude and, in a sense, most older children and adults are "language problems."

For example, recall the case of the boy described earlier who was bilingual as a baby, and who later had difficulty learning to read. During his early formative years, his brain could and did record the auditory imagery of both English and German and reproduce the accents of both. If as an adult he tried to learn another language, such as French, it would take years—if it were to happen at all—before he would be able to say French words without English sounds. In other words, his brain would have such difficulty in acquiring new auditory imagery, that it would be forced to use established pathways. These English sound images would give him his English accent. As a child he mastered two languages effortlessly. As an adult he is a "language problem."

It is quite clear that, in order to acquire the auditory imagery of language most easily, the brain must be exposed before the age of six to the sounds of that language. What has not been realized is that with the visual imagery of printed language, the same early exposure is necessary. As we have pointed out, the child has a language aptitude before six and this faculty enables him to master the imagery of languages in his environment. It does not matter whether the symbol-images are printed or spoken, for where the brain has sufficient exposure under meaningful conditions it will master the import of the symbols. The critical point to grasp for an understanding of our reading problems is that, while we have recognized the child's need for extremely early exposure to aural language, we have not recognized the parallel need for just as early an exposure to visual language.

Early establishment of sensory imagery is an essential part of all language development, visual or aural. This can be seen most clearly by reviewing again the three stages in the communication process.

The first is the sensational or sensory level in which an impression is made on one of the senses. For example, let us consider the first impression which is made by an unfamiliar object. Initially, we experience only a vague, confused sense of the figure-ground relationship. Then, if the experience is sustained, we are able to gradually form a clear image of the object. This is the second, or perceptual level. At this stage, particular patterns of electro-chemical impulses have been recorded in the brain and experienced as images. This can be illustrated by a situation in which students are able to recognize words in a foreign language which they do not comprehend as symbols. The third stage is the cognitive act by which the perceptual image is recognized as a symbol. It requires the highest level of human intelligence to recognize the symbolic import of a visual image.

The written word, then, is first a pattern of light waves that is projected on the photoreceptor cells of the retina; then it is an electro-chemical impulse sent to the brain, where it is recorded as a visual image and matched with existing images in the memory banks for meaning. Last, it is interpreted as a symbol with meaning beyond its perceptual image.

In the process of learning to read, the child must master all three stages. First, his sensory pathways must mature to a point where they can respond to the stimulus. Second, his visual-perceptual areas in the brain must develop engrams, or traces, which will enable him to recognize the shape as an image. Third, his cognitive faculties must grasp the relationship between the graphic form as a symbol and the object, person or action to which it refers. The chronology of the development of these faculties in the central nervous system is of great importance, and, with reference to the reading problems, it is the second or perceptual phase which explains the origins of the difficulty.

For years it was assumed by many that vision matured more or less independently with reference to experience and environment. It was not thought that vision had to be learned and that seeing was more than just "opening the eyes." Research in several related fields has altered this conception, but two areas of investigation which have been particularly influential are (1) animals reared in darkness, and (2) persons born blind who subsequently gain sight. When these subjects had been exposed to light by an experimenter's design or, as in the case of the congenitally blind, by operation, rather surprising discoveries were made.

The classical concept of maturation as an independent, internal process would lead us to expect that these subjects, upon attaining sight, would rapidly develop normal vision. Such, in fact, is not the case, for as several studies with animals reared in darkness have shown, the deprived animals have required extended periods of practice before they achieved efficiency in the performance of normal visual tasks.[1] In summarizing some of the implications from these studies, J. McV. Hunt noted:

> ... these experiments confirm those described earlier showing that all of the experimental animals reared in darkness were much inferior to normally reared animals in the original acquisition of such a discrimination (a black triangle from a circle). A

background of primary visual learning is apparently necessary before visual discriminations can be acquired.[2]

The research with the congenitally blind who recover sight in adulthood is of even greater interest. Doctor M. von Senden, a German psychologist, has done extensive work with these problems.[3] His data demonstrate the great efforts which these persons must make in order to gain even a modest mastery of their visual environment. He records the difficulty they have in learning to recognize shapes and colors and in developing visual memory, or imagery, and visual fantasy. Even some time after gaining sight, they still depended on touch to identify small objects. For example, in order to distinguish a triangle and a square *they found it necessary to count the angles.* This last feat, incidentally, can be accomplished by the normal infant sometime between six months and one year.[4] Infants with no concept of geometrical form can learn to recognize shapes after a number of trials, but adults born blind and gaining sight after childhood find the task extremely difficult.

Though studies of this sort, taken alone, do not constitute final proof, it appears most likely that the child's brain is superior to the adults' in the development of visual imagery. To use an analogy, one might say that the brain is in some respects like a computer: It can only work with the programs stored in its memory banks. Moreover, in the case of the brain there is a period when certain kinds of programs must be stored, or the "brain-computer" will never have access to them. One category of such programs appears to be sensory imagery. When the brain is deprived of exposure to this imagery in its absorbent period, it becomes permanently limited in its avenues of expression. In acquiring new information, it must depend to a great extent on these early programs of sensory imagery. After five, the brain finds it increasingly difficult to learn directly from the environment.

The origins of an inability to handle visual language forms in the reading problem, then, parallels, at a perceptual level, the difficulty that the adult has in mastering the aural imagery of a foreign language. We have always understood that if language exposure does not occur before the age of six, the new language would be learned as a variation of the mother tongue and would be, to some extent, deficient in accent. Accent reflects the perceptual imagery of language in the brain, and the presence of an accent of one language in the spoken expression of another is a clear manifestation of an underlying inability to form clear auditory images of the second language. Adults, who have difficulty perceiving many of the sounds that are part of the pronunciation of another language, will have difficulty reproducing these sounds.

However, in the adult mastering a language, the presence of some perceptual blind spots does not block his eventual degree of mastery of the language, but with the poor reading student, the inability to formulate clear imagery occurs in a sensory modality where he has no established system of language imagery which can, through analogy, subserve his perceptual limitations. The reading problem who finds the letters and the words twisting about, and who confuses the configuration of words which appear somewhat alike has no substrata of visual language forms upon which to fall back for assistance. In learning a foreign language, the adult has the assistance of his native tongue which, analogous to the new language, enables him to overcome the blocks in language imagery to a great extent.

Even the first grade student who may eventually master reading, has special problems as he first approaches the printed symbol. He is out of his period of language sensitivity and must struggle to imprint on his brain the minute and complex forms of graphic language. Under ideal conditions, the perceptual forms of words constructed from the graphic would be difficult,[5] but occurring during a period when many children have lost, or are losing, their eidetic memory and the plasticity of their central nervous systems, the difficulties are compounded. By the age of six, most children are out of the stage when simple forms and shapes arouse their curiosity, when mere repetition of sights and sounds delight them. As Montessori stressed some years ago, by the age of six many children are beginning to explore relationships between areas of experience, and the interest and satisfaction they displayed earlier for the rote naming of parts is gone.

Moreover, while the child of two or three can memorize quantities of sounds and sights, however arbitrary and unrelated they may be, the older child, who lacks a precedent for "visual" words, can no longer memorize the new forms "automatically" and tends to fall back upon his existing system of auditory images. Only by translating the visual into the auditory is he able to "see" and "say" himself through the "alien" graphic forms. In a sense, the novice reader is translating the foreign language, "reading," into his native tongue, "speech." In varying degrees, this "inner speech" characterizes the vast majority of readers. Even when, during the height of popularity of the sight recognition method attempts were made to teach children to read without sounding out the words, the tendency to subvocalize appeared just as frequently among these "sight trained" readers.

The severe functional reading problems are those who never successfully establish sufficient visual imagery to provide a ground for association with their already established auditory imagery. They cannot organize the visual imagery of words well enough to take advantage of their established speech patterns. These individuals are very poor readers who become increasingly dependent on aural language as a compensation for their limitations with visual imagery. Edward Dolch, who strongly advocated sight recognition in reading instruction, made precisely this point in his *Manual for Remedial Reading*. In a section headed, "Oral Reading Helps Most," he commented:

> The greatest help for the poor readers in any class group is to have the textbook lessons read aloud, whatever the subject may be. . . . First of all, poor readers tend to be "ear learners." That is, they understand and remember what they hear better than what they read, perhaps because most of their learning has been by ear.[6]

But the reason that they are "ear learners" is the key which gives us insight into the whole matter of reading problems among normal children. Reading authorities generally have not understood the importance of early exposure to visual symbols. It is this exposure which explains why reading problems find the imagery of aural language, the language of their formative period, most meaningful. The failure to understand the role of sensitive learning periods is also at the root of the confusion in the controversy over phonic and sight recognition reading instruction.

SUMMARY

To exploit the brain's early sensitivity to sensory forms, we must expose the child to both aural and visual language. In beginning reading, the child must master the three stages of the communication process: sensory, perceptual and cognitive. Extensive experiments with birds and animals reared under conditions of darkness indicate that normal visual functioning must be learned. Von Senden's investigations of individuals who were born blind but later recovered sight reinforce the findings of the animal laboratory. These persons had trouble learning to recognize even "simple" shapes.

The adult finds it difficult if not impossible to learn a foreign language without some accent. The child who is past his sensitive period for the establishment of visual imagery will experience varying degrees of difficulty mastering language in graphic form. He will tend to rely upon the aural imagery which he has learned earlier. The functional reading problem has failed to program his "brain-computer" with the necessary visual imagery for mastering graphic language.

REFERENCES

1. HUNT, J. McV.: *Intelligence and Experience.* New York, Ronald Press, 1961, p. 92.
2. *Ibid.,* p. 96.
3. VON SENDEN, M.: *Space and Sight: The Perception of Space and Shape in the Congenitally Blind Before and After Operation.* Translated by Peter Heath. New York, Free Press of Glencoe, 1960, p. 348.
4. LING, BING C.: Form discrimination as a learning cue in infants. *Comparative Psychology Monographs, 17,* 1941.
5. MONEY, JOHN, (ED.): Dyslexia: A Postconference Review. *Reading Disability,* Baltimore, The Johns Hopkins Press, pp. 22-25, 1962.
6. DOLCH, EDWARD W.: *A Manual for Remedial Reading.* 2nd Ed., 9th print. Champaign, Ill., The Garrard Press, pp. 206-208, 1957.

SUGGESTED READINGS, BRIEFLY ANNOTATED

1. BEACH, F.: Early experience and the behavior of animals. *Psychological Bulletin, 51,* 1954.

A review of the research on the effect of early experience on behavior, including references to the work of Harlow (learning sets), Hebb (early learning and adult performance), and Siegel, (experiments with hooded ring doves.)

2. BUSWELL, G.: The process of reading. *The Reading Teacher,* 1959.

Buswell sees reading instruction in first grade as perceptual in nature, not conceptual. Conceptual language is already established through speech. "The teaching of reading is basically a problem of visual perception."

  3. DOLCH, E.: *A Manual for Remedial Reading.* 2nd Ed. Champaign, Ill., Gerrard Press, 1946.

Dolch's second step in the process of remedial reading involves building sight vocabulary and speeding up recognition.

  4. FRIES, C.: *Linguistics and Reading.* New York, Holt, Rinehart & Winston, 1962.

Fries points out that the normal child acquires his spoken mastery of language with little formal instruction and there is no obvious reason to believe that such fluency should not be readily reproduced with "visual" language. Fries advocates that we parallel the method by which spoken language is acquired in the teaching of reading.

  5. FRYMIER, J.: Relationship of aural perceptions to cultural situations. *Perceptual and Motor Skills,* 8:67-70, 1958.

Subjects from different cultural situations tend to perceive the same sounds differently.

  6. GORELICK, M.: The effectiveness of visual form training in a prereading program. *The Journal of Educational Research,* 58:315-318, 1965.

"Reading readiness" programs should include opportunities for children to practice the visual discrimination of words.

  7. HARLOW, HARRY: The evolution of learning. *Behavior and Evolution,* Edited by Roe, A., and Simpson, G., New Haven, Yale University Press, 1958.

Harlow and his associates have shown experimentally how children and lower primates develop "learning sets" in the solution of discrimination and other problems. Data indicate that human and subhuman animals must literally learn to think. Thinking is not a spontaneous development of innate abilities, but rather, the culmination of a long process.

This selection contains references to some of his other titles. See also Harlow, H.: The formation of learning sets. *Psychological Review,* 56:51-65, 1949.

  8. HEBB, D.: *The Organization of Behavior; A Neuropsychological Approach.* New York, Wiley, 2nd print., 1952.

This book has had a major influence on psychology, and learning theory in particular. Hebb, from his work in animal psychology, develops a theory of the role of early developmental learning experiences as determining adult animal learning capacity. Though starting with the extensive work done in animal neurophysiology and animal psychology, Hebb brings together available evidence on the nature of the development of the human central nervous system.

9. HOLMES, J.: The brain and the reading process. *Claremont College Reading Conference, 22nd Yearbook,* Claremont, Calif., Claremont College, 1957.

A cogent discussion of the neurological basis of reading and reading disability.

10. KOTTMEYER, W.: *Teacher's Guide for Remedial Reading.* St. Louis, Webster Publishing Co., 1959.

"Whatever the pattern of causative factors may be among remedial pupils, a common characteristic appears among them: varying degrees of inability to use basic word perception techniques. Almost ninety-five per cent of our clinic cases are in this category." (p. 22)

11. PETTY, M.: An experimental study of certain factors influencing reading readiness. *Journal of Educational Psychology, 30*: 215-230, 1939.

An attempt to relate eidetic imagery to success in beginning reading.

12. SOLOMON, P., et al. (ED.): *Sensory Deprivation: A Symposium Held at Harvard Medical School.* Cambridge, Mass., Harvard University Press, 1961.

The Introduction is largely concerned with acknowledging the courageous pioneering role of Hebb in crystallizing interest in sensory deprivation and many other phenomena. Such topics as "sensory distortion" and "sensory overload" are discussed.

13. TERRELL, G., and WARE, R.: Role of delay of reward in speed of size and form discrimination learning in childhood. *Child Development, 32*:409-415, 1961.

A report of the relative effects of a delayed reward and an immediate reward (light flash) in two experiments involving size and form discrimination learning problems. Forty Ss, kindergartners and first-graders were used in each experiment. In both experiments, Ss learned significantly more quickly when rewarded following a delay of seven seconds.

14. WILSON, F., FLEMMING, C., BURKE, A., and GARRISON, C.: Reading progress in kindergarten and primary grades, *Elementary School Journal, 38*:442-449, 1938.

This study emphasizes the interest children have in letters. Children who knew the most letter forms and sounds tended to be among the first to learn to read, and to be the best readers.

15. WILSON, F., and FLEMMING, C.: Correlations of reading progress with other abilities and traits of grade I. *Journal of Genetic Psychology, 53*:33-35, 1938.

The authors conclude that "ability with letters" is more closely

related to reading achievement than various abilities studied, and that this relationship is not due to mental age or IQ.
>   16. WERNER, H., and KAPLAN, E.: *The Acquisition of Word Meanings: A Developmental Study*. Monograph of the Society for Research in Child Development, Inc. 15, Northwestern University, Evanston, Illinois, Society for Research in Child Development, Inc., 1952.

A study to investigate experimentally the processes underlying the acquisition of word meaning through verbal context using artificial words embedded in sentences, employing a total of 125 boys and girls aged 8-13.

ADDITIONAL READINGS

1. BIJOU, S., and STURGES, P.: Positive reinforcers for experimental studies with children—consumables and manipulatables. *Child Development, 30*:151-170, 1959.
2. BRUNER, J.: Neural mechanisms in perception. *Psychological Review, 64*:340-58, 1957.
3. HAMILTON, F.: *The Perceptual Factors in Reading*. Columbia University Contributions to Philosophy, Psychology, and Education, 17, New York, Science Press, 1907.
4. HESS, E.: Imprinting in animals. *Scientific American*, 1958, pp. 81-90.
5. HOLMES, J., and SINGER, H.: Theoretical models and trends toward more basic research in reading. *Review of Educational Research, 34*:127, 1964.
6. ITARD, J.: *The Wild Boy of Aveyron*. Translated by G. and M. Humphrey. New York and London, Century, 1932.
7. LEEPER, R.: A study of a neglected portion of the field of learning—development of sensory organization. *Journal of Genetic Psychology, 46*:41-75, 1935.
8. SHEPARD, W.: Learning set in preschool children. *Journal of Comparative and Physiological Psychology, 50*:15-17, 1957.
9. STAATS, A.: The conditioning of textual responses using "Extrinsic" Reinforcers. *Journal of the Experimental Analysis of Behavior, 5*, 1962.
10. THOMPSON, WILLIAM: Early Environment—Its Importance for Later Behavior. In *Psychopathology of Childhood*, edited by Hoch, Paul, and Zubin, Joseph. New York, Grune & Stratton, 1955.

Chapter Seven

SIGHT AND SOUND IN READING

MAIN POINTS

The "sight recognition"—phonic method controversy.
Flaws in the popular concept of "reading readiness."
Importance of timing in "sight recognition" approach to reading instruction.
Why phonics works remedially.
Proficient readers' lack of dependence upon auditory imagery.
The cultural error of type size.
Reading readiness as perceptual readiness.
Child's language readiness begins during first year.
Why reading could precede speech.
Very young child should be exposed to visual symbols appropriately graded in size and complexity.

As Gray has noted, the teaching of reading in the United States since 1900 has swung from one extreme to another.

By 1920, the revolt against the old "phonic" readers reached such proportions that: "In many schools, teachers were sternly warned by their superiors against giving any special attention to the visual forms of words whether by sight or by phonetic methods, as a preparation for reading."[1]

"Reading for Meaning" became the catch-phrase, as children, paradoxically, were expected to identify new words by "guessing" from context.

Says Gray:

> The results of the extreme viewpoints, however, were dramatized in the thirties and early forties in certain towns and cities by groups of young people who were disinterested and inefficient in reading, by the anomaly of intelligent illiterates in high

schools, and by large high-school remedial programs which attempted to correct the lack of systematic teaching in the early grades.[2]

Today, as Greenman has indicated, the controversy over the respective roles of sight recognition and phonics in beginning reading has not yet been resolved by educators, and the public senses this difference in opinion regarding the so-called "sight word" and phonic approaches:

"As long as a large segment of the professional educators in the field of reading insists that the initial reading experiences must involve the building of sight vocabulary, and other educators say phonics can be introduced and applied prior to memorizing any group of words by sight, this difference of opinion will continue . . ."[3]

Some advocates of the sight recognition method point out that phonic instruction which emphasizes the sound value of letters and syllables tends to produce very slow readers whose ability to sound out words by no means necessarily reflects satisfactory comprehension of the ideas expressed. And at the same time, they have noted that very good readers read by sight, grasping phrases rather than words, and do not sound out words or subvocalize as much as their slower classmates. These skillful readers deal directly with the idea-content of the word patterns without resorting to the word-by-word mechanics of speech. Many investigators concluded, then, that sight recognition was the proper method of learning to read and that the phonics approach was unnatural and could be detrimental.

However, perceptive teachers have protested for years that sight recognition did not work well, if at all, for some of their children. Such teachers have often fallen back upon the phonics method, whatever its limitations, arguing that even if a child learns to read subvocally and slowly, he is at least reading.

In recent decades, the concept of readiness has been widely used to account for great numbers of poor readers. Reading readiness is commonly held to be a certain level of physical, psychological, intellectual, and social maturity which the child must attain before he can learn to read. According to the "readiness concept," the child who is experiencing great difficulty in learning to read is probably not ready to read. He has not reached the requisite level of maturity in one or more of the four areas mentioned. Though the "readiness" idea has become very popular, actual research and practice has provided little evidence to support it. Of late, many psychologists and teachers have become skeptical and even openly critical of "readiness" as traditionally understood. Doctor Donald Durrell of Boston University, in his books and in several articles, has underscored the flaws in the readiness notion. For example, he says:

> Apparently we forget that large amounts of specific learning have taken place in the preschool years. Some children come to school able to read well in a primer; others cannot tell the capital letters apart. Some can write words from memory, using lower-case letters, while others cannot copy block capitals accurately. The rate of learning to read seems to relate more closely to background skill of this type than to mental age. The remedy for lack of reading readiness consists in giving the child specific backgrounds for reading rather than "waiting until he is ready."[4]

As Doctor Charles Fries, Professor Emeritus of the University of Michigan has observed, historically most of the early teaching of the reading process occurred in the home rather than in school. "Even today," he notes, "some of the best-known private schools of England—schools which receive pupils of five years of age—will not accept those of this age who cannot already read."[5]

Fries and his wife wrote a little book for a three-year-old boy as long ago as 1940, and they have successfully taught children of three and four reading.[6]

Where the concept of readiness has been stressed, teachers and parents have often been assured optimistically that if they waited long enough, the child would eventually achieve readiness, and would begin to learn to read naturally and easily. However, in many cases the longer they waited the worse the problem became. Teachers and parents found themselves with adolescents who were in all other respects normal, but who could not read, and who gave little evidence that they would ever be ready.

Objections were raised by other educators and concerned citizens. High school and college teachers and businessmen protested that many students were inadequate readers. The mass of substandard readers were coupled with another less serious but irritating problem. Many of the sight trained readers had difficulty with spelling. Now, while English is at best a very hard language to learn to spell, about 75 per cent of its words are phonetic. Phonic-trained readers of the past could spell the "regular" words with some ease. Many of the sight readers demonstrated no such ability, and articles in national magazines and newspapers were soon calling attention to the fact that our school system was producing poor spellers.

Recent decades have seen a spate of articles and books criticizing the sight method and demanding a return to phonics. At the present time something of a compromise has been worked out, with a combination of sight recognition, phonics and other approaches to beginning reading being employed.

From the point of view of this book, both the champions of word recognition, and of phonics are right and wrong at the same time. Ironically, everything claimed for sight recognition techniques as a method for reading instruction is correct; it is the timing which is out of phase. By waiting until six, the reading teacher is trying to stimulate "memory banks" that are no longer so readily accessible. And, of course, the phonics advocates are correct in maintaining that the best approach for the average six year old is to base visual language skills on his existing auditory mastery of language. The sight recognition school is wrong for the right reasons and the phonics school is right for the wrong reasons.

With this perspective in mind, it is easy to understand the success that remedial techniques employing phonics have had with deficient readers. Naturally, if these students with limited ability to organize visual imagery are going to cope with language, they will do so best on an auditory basis. Because speech is native to their brains, they function best when they are trained to translate the visual images of reading into the auditory imagery of speech. Even the normal reader tends to do this most of the time, and for the same reasons. Few of us are as at home with visual symbols as we are with auditory ones.

By way of contrast, it is worth noting that very proficient readers, who read with great speed and accuracy, report very little auditory imagery in their reading. In fact, developmental reading courses designed to improve the speed and comprehension of normal readers have always had as a prime objective the reduction of subvocalization in the reading process. It has been the experience of developmental reading specialists that readers who can reduce their dependence on auditory imagery read much faster and better than do the readers who are dependent upon "silent speech." Finally, it is of interest to note that studies of superior readers shows that a high percentage of them have had pre-school reading experience.[7]

From our point of view, then, reading problems are not "reading" problems in the strictest sense, but perceptual problems. If we recognize that the essence of the language process is the ability to interpret symbols, the functional reading problem is not cognitionally deficient. It is not a matter of his inability to comprehend symbols, but the absence of an early experiential ground of perceptual fluency out of which to formulate visual symbols which limits him.

This points up a major shortcoming of written intelligence tests, for whether one is dealing with the retarded reader or the average reader, any printed test is measuring not only cognition but also perceptual proficiency. To restate the analogy we have already employed, written tests are, for many of us, tests in a "foreign" language. Verbal or auditory tests would often provide a much better measure of innate intelligence. This is often so because spoken symbols are, for many, if not most persons, more native than printed words.

In attempting to determine reading readiness in children, educational theorists have fallen into a trap. This trap has been the artificial nature of written symbols in our society. Writing and reading evolved as adult tasks, and the form in which we put these symbols reflects the visual maturity of the adult brain. There is no question that the adult can make finer prolonged figure-ground discriminations at near point than the young child.[8,9] There is no question that words printed in 8 or 10 point type and crowded together in the format of the page present a most difficult perceptual task for the inexperienced child. But, one must ask, what does this have to do with the essence of the reading act? Reading represents the capacity of the brain to form visual images and interpret their symbolic import. The size of type necessary to stimulate the brain and evoke the language faculty is a secondary consideration. Reading experts who have used some measure of visual maturity as a criterion for reading readiness have failed to detect the "cultural" error. They have assumed that the size of the type used in printing was somehow natural. They have failed to recognize that type size is a product of historical circumstances and has no necessary "neurological" significance. It may be true, as so many reading experts have pointed out, that small children cannot perceive small letters comfortably; but it is also true that very young children do not understand mumbled or whispered words easily either. We do not consider delaying speech until the child is six just because he appears to have less auditory acuity for words than do adults. If we did we would certainly have just as many listening problems as we now have reading problems.

Much of the discussion of reading readiness is really a discussion of "perceptual readiness." It is only a historical circumstance that visual language symbols came to be written in small characters, bunched together and hidden between the covers of closed books. The relative size of the letters has nothing to do with the symbolic import of the words. Whether the words are small or large, they have the same meaning. The fact that very young children cannot easily perceive fine type places no restriction on their ability to understand symbols, any more than the presbyopia of the older adult means that he is a reading problem. Both the child and the adult have the same functional problem: they cannot perceive fine print. We correct one with lenses and we can compensate for the other with very large print. Let us not confuse immature visual faculties with readiness to receive and comprehend visual symbols. The language faculty is a central process that depends on information received through sensory pathways. As long as the brain is getting a clear signal, it can function. The sensory pathways only report data to the brain, and it is the brain, and the brain only, that interprets the data.

This brings us back to our question, "When is the child ready to read?" The answer is clear. Whenever the child's brain responds to language through any one of the major sensory systems, it is ready to respond through all of them. To conclude anything else would be to imply the existence of a "language center" in the ear drum or some such impossible notion.

Between six months and one year, the normal child begins to understand language; that is, he begins to recognize that certain sounds refer to objects, actions, and persons in his environment. By the age of one, he is usually attempting to reproduce these sounds. If we recognize the central nature of the language learning process, we must conclude that the child should be exposed similarly to visual symbols graded in size and complexity to his level of maturity during this same period.

This suggests that, in theory, a child could begin recognizing words visually before he began reproducing them orally, that he could read before he talks. Though this may appear incredible, it is really the same process that we have all witnessed in the child's speech development. Children always master language aurally before they can reproduce it orally. With visual language, it should be the same; the reception of symbols could take place in the brain long before the child could begin to express symbols.

Because, historically, oral language developed before visual language, we have assumed that the sequence had some neurological or biological basis, and that children should be exposed to reading after speech has been established. However, the great weight of evidence from recent studies in perception, learning psychology, and neurology, which is briefly covered in this book, indicates that language development is a central process capable of responding to any sensory presentation that is clear and consistent. The popular notion of reading readiness which has obscured the teaching of reading for some years is, in fact, a misunderstanding which developed as the result of inaccurate cultural assumptions. There is no "reading" readiness in the child, only a "language" readiness. This language readiness begins to function sometime in the first year of life.

By focusing attention on physical, psychological, intellectual or social maturity, many students of reading have been led away from any real understanding of the language aptitude in the child. By waiting until the child is "ready to read," we are delaying the introduction of a language skill that should be acquired early in life. The child, in order to realize his full potential, must have early exposure to the perceptual forms of visual language. There is only one period when imagery can be most readily developed—before the age of six. After that sensitive stage is over, most people have very limited ability to acquire sensory imagery. It is not our children who have reading problems but our society which does not understand the nature of the child's language development process.

SUMMARY

The "sight recognition"—phonics controversy in this country, which has seen shifts from one extreme to another, continues.

Sight recognition methodology has much to recommend it if employed during the child's sensitive period for establishing visual imagery—from birth to about age six. When this period has passed, phonics techniques become increasingly necessary. The utilization of auditory imagery in phonics suits this approach for remedial work.

The popular concept of "reading readiness" is in error. Rather than wait for "reading readiness," the teacher should guide the child to initial steps in beginning reading.

Superior readers, many of whom interestingly learned to read before entering school, demonstrate a lack of dependence upon auditory imagery.

Functional reading problems are perceptual problems, and reading readiness is perceptual readiness. The child is actually ready for exposure to all language forms in his earliest years. However, these language forms should be appropriately scaled to the young learner. The aural symbols of speech should be loud enough and clear. The visual symbols of graphic language must also be "loud" (large) enough and clear.

REFERENCES

1. GRAY, WILLIAM: *On Their Own in Reading.* Chicago, Scott, Foresman, p. 26, 1948.
2. *Ibid.,* p. 27.
3. GREENMAN, MARGARET: A minority report. *Learning to Read: A Report of a Conference of Reading Experts.* Princeton, Educational Testing Service, pp. 23-24, 1962.
4. DURRELL, DONALD: Learning difficulties among children of normal intelligence. *Elementary School Journal,* 55: 1954.
5. FRIES, CHARLES: *Linguistics and Reading.* New York, Holt, Rinehart and Winston, p. 2, 1962.
6. *Ibid.,* p. XI.
7. KASDON, LAWRENCE: Early reading background of some superior

readers among college freshmen. *Journal of Educational Research,* 52:151-153, 1958.
8. SCHUBERT, DELWYN: Visual immaturity and reading difficulty. *Elementary English,* pp. 323-52, 1957.
9. BERNER, G., and BERNER, D.: Reading difficulties in children. *Archives of Opthalmology,* 20:830, 1938.

ADDITIONAL READINGS

1. ATTNEAVE, F.: Symmetry, information and memory for patterns. *American Journal of Psychology,* 68:209-222, 1955.
2. ATTNEAVE, F., and ARNOULT, M.: The quantitative study of shape and pattern perception. *Psychological Bulletin,* 53:452-471, 1956.
3. ANDERSON, M., and LEONARD, J.: The recognition, naming, and reconstruction of visual figures as a function of contour redundancy. *Journal of Experimental Psychology,* 56:262-270, 1958.
4. BEVAN, W., and ZENER, K.: Some influences of past experience upon the perceptual thresholds of visual form. *American Journal of Psychology,* 65:434-442, 1952.
5. BLOOMFIELD, L., and BARNHART, C.: *Let's Read: A Linguistic Approach,* Detroit, Wayne State University Press, 1961.
6. BONEY, C.: Teaching children to read as they learned to talk. *Elementary English Review,* 16:139ff., 1939.
7. BROWN, R.: How shall a thing be called? *Psychological Review,* 65: 14-21, 1958.
8. CARROLL, J.: Linguistics and the psychology of language. *Review of Educational Research: Language Arts and Fine Arts.* 34:119, 1964.
9. DURKIN, D.: Linguistics and the teaching of reading. *The Reading Teacher,* 16:342-346, 1964.
10. FORGAYS: The development of differential word recognition. *Journal of Experimental Psychology,* 45:165-168, 1953.
11. GIBSON, ELEANOR J., and WALK R.: The effect of prolonged exposure to visually presented patterns on learning to discriminate them. *Journal of Comparative and Physiological Psychology,* 49:239-242, 1956.
12. GIBSON, E.: A systematic application of the concept of generalization and differentiation to verbal learning. *Psychological Review.* 47: 206, 1940.
13. GOODMAN, K.: A communicative theory of the reading curriculum. *Elementary English,* 40:290-298, 1963.
14. LEFEVRE, C.: Linguistics and the teaching of reading. *Reading as an Intellectual Activity: International Reading Association Conference Proceedings,* 8:188, 1963.
15. MILLS, R.: An evaluation of techniques for teaching word recognition. *Elementary School Journal,* 56:221-25, 1956.

16. Mowrer, O.: The psychologist looks at language. *American Psychologist, 9*:660-694, 1954.
17. Pratt, C.: The role of past experience in visual perception. *Journal of Psychology, 30*:85-107, 1950.
18. Rappaport, M.: The role of redundancy in the discrimination of visual forms. *Journal of Experimental Psychology, 53*:3-10, 1957.
19. Renshaw, S.: Reading as a special case of perception. *Visual Digest, 5*: 1941.
20. Secor, W.: Visual reading: a study in mental imagery. *American Journal of Psychology, 11*:225-36, 1900.
21. Spence, K.W.: The nature of discrimination learning in animals. *Psychological Review, 43*:427-449, 1936.
22. Steigman, M., and Stevenson, H.: The effect of pretraining reinforcement schedules on children's learning. *Child Development, 31*:53-59.
23. Tolman, E.: Cognitive maps in rats and men. *Psychological Review, 55*:189-208, 1948.
24. Welch, L.: The development of discrimination of form and area. *Journal of Psychology, 7*:37-54, 1939.
25. Welch, L.: The development of size discrimination between the ages of 12 and 40 months. *Journal of Genetic Psychology, 55*:243-268, 1939.
26. Woodworth, R.: Reinforcement of perception. *The American Journal of Psychology, 60*:119-124, 1947.

Chapter Eight

MONTESSORI AND EARLY LEARNING*

MAIN POINTS

Montessori's concept of "sensitive periods."
The sensitive period for language.
The need for a "prepared environment" language-wise.
The child's power of concentration.
Unique absorptive mentality of childhood.
Child's direct language learning.
Child learner in contrast to adult learner.
Role of educator is to prepare environment sensitive to child's needs.

MONTESSORI'S EXPERIENCES with young children in the "prepared environment" of her "Houses of Childhood" convinced her that, *given the opportunity,* children will reveal unforeseen learning capacities. Observations of children in the restricted environment of the traditional classroom do not, she felt, give a true picture of the child's potential or the nature of the learning process in the very young child.

She refers to the accumulated prejudices and vested interests concerning the child. "I mean above all," she says, "the interest created in protecting children from 'mental effort,' 'precocious intellectual activity,' etc."[1]

Many teachers, Montessori asserted, have a prejudiced notion concerning fatigue in the child. "A child who is interested in what

---
*Stevens, George: Montessori and early intellectual education. In *A Montessori Handbook*, Ed. by R. C. Orem, New York, Putnam, 1965, p. 130. "The early development of intellectual skills such as reading and writing has become a subject of major concern during the present period. Yet, Maria Montessori developed concepts and classroom practices which actually produced 'early readers' among the underprivileged children of an Italian slum more than half a century ago.

he is doing goes on and on without fatigue, but when the teacher makes him change every few minutes and rest, he loses interest and gets fatigued."[2]

Montessori's studies indicate that the child in process of development passes through a series of what she termed "sensitive periods"—times of special receptivity to certain learnings.

"If in education one takes into due consideration these sensitive periods, one may sometimes arrive at results which are surprising and, above all, contradictory to our prejudices concerning the uniform progression of the intellect, and our ideas with regard to fatigue in learning."[3]

A sensitive period is a base for acquisitions which the individual will no longer be able to gain at a later age. "It is during the sensitive period," says Montessori, "that a function can be more perfectly established, or an ability can be acquired in a more perfect manner."[4]

Montessori stresses the importance of allowing the child to utilize his sensitive periods, for they are transitory in nature and once gone, cannot be recaptured.

"Thus, in the early acquisition of sense impressions . . . there are periods in childhood which, if they pass without bearing fruit, can never be replaced in their effects."[5]

The child displays a long sensitive period, lasting "almost to the age of five," during which he has "a truly prodigious capacity" for "possessing itself of the images of its environment."[6] His sensitivity during this time "leads him to absorb everything about him."[7]

So the first period of life, then, is one of storing impressions from the environment. The first five years constitute the sensitive period for language development. Says Montessori:

> The development of language continues in fact, up to the age of five years, and the mind during this period is in a phase of activity regarding everything that has to do with words.[8]

During this time, the child should be exposed to exemplary language in its various forms:

"Many adults must have noticed the intense attention given by children to the conversation of grown-ups when they cannot possibly be understanding a word of what they hear. They are trying to get hold of words . . ."[9]

If we are to help the child we must keep him with us, "so that he can see what we do and hear what we say."[10]

We have noted earlier that if the child is given the opportunity to express his potential during a sensitive period, the results may be quite surprising, far exceeding the norms of traditional educational expectations. For example, children who are given the materials and preparation for writing during the sensitive period for this skill will achieve more than if writing is postponed.

"Children who are able to commence writing at the proper age (i.e., four-and-a-half or five years of age) reach a perfection in writing which you will not find in children who have begun to write at six or seven; but especially you will not find in this later stage that enthusiasm and the richness of production . . ."[11]

Montessori realized that every child needs responsive, orderly surroundings in which he can discover the materials necessary for his self-development. The child needs *freedom*, but he also needs the *organization of work* which a *prepared environment* offers. The child, according to Montessori, "*makes himself* out of the elements of his environment."[12] Since the child can only develop fully by means of what she termed "experiences on the environment," it is vitally important that we "prepare the environment in a definite manner," offering the child "the external means directly necessary for him."[13]

Once the environment has been prepared, the directress will find that even the very young child's "span of attention" is anything but short.

"The directress should not, however, become alarmed even if the children give themselves up exclusively for several days to one kind of work; this is what we call an 'explosion' . . . this continuous application to one kind of work . . ."[14]

She speaks of the "explosion into language," noting that we may "see a child occupied for seven or eight days with the same work."[15]

Such concentration should not puzzle the adult for ". . . the child's love of knowledge is such that it surpasses every other love . . ."[16] Therefore, "intellectual exercise is the most pleasing of all to the small child if he is in good health."[17]

Montessori notes that if we call our adult mentality "conscious," then we must call the child's "unconscious." Adults who tend to think of the child's mentality as inferior are mistaken. "An unconscious mind can be most intelligent."[18]

It could be said that we acquire knowledge by "using our minds," but, in contrast, "the child absorbs knowledge directly into his psychic life."[19]

Says Montessori:

> Like a sponge these children absorb. It is marvellous this mental power of the child. Only we cannot teach directly. It is necessary that the child teach himself, and then the success is great.[20]

Montessori describes the child as a "worker and a producer." The adult's work is external, and is usually connected with the production of marketable goods or services.

The child has his own work too, but it is internal—"a great, important, difficult work indeed—the work of producing man."[21]

The child's "power" then, lies in his capacity for self-development. In the space of a few years, he is able to build a personality and to adapt to whatever the demands of the culture and geography may be. "The child," says Montessori, "builds his inmost self out of the deeply felt impressions he receives." Especially important, then, are the impressions of the early years of his life, for "nothing that has been formed in infancy can ever be wholly eradicated."[22] Montessori speaks of the infant's task of adaption. He must "construct a model of behavior which renders him free to act in the world about him and to influence it."[23]

To this task, the child brings his unique absorptive mentality. "There exists in the small child an unconscious mental state which is of a creative nature. We have called it the 'Absorbent Mind.'"[24]

Montessori speaks of the "two different personalities in the child and the adult."[25] It is not a question of a minimum growing gradually to a maximum, for the child has his own unique psychological characteristics. These characteristics "are not those of the adult reduced to a diminutive scale."[26]

There is a "mental form" unique to childhood, which is only now being recognized. Observation of the child's language learning proves that the child possesses "special psychic powers." Says Montessori:

Our mind, as it is, would not be able to do what the child's mind does. To develop a language from nothing needs a different type of mentality. This the child has. His intelligence is not of the same kind as ours.[27]

We have already noted that human language is the most complex and remarkable of man's achievements. Yet, as Montessori notes:

By merely 'living' and without any conscious effort the individual absorbs from the environment even a complex cultural achievement like language.[28]

According to her, "Only the child under three can construct the mechanism of language, and he can speak any number of languages, if they are in his environment at birth."[29]

Furthermore, "The mother tongue alone is well pronounced because it was established in the period of childhood; and the adult who learns to speak a new language must bring to it the imperfections characteristic of the foreigner's speech . . . thus also the *defects* acquired in childhood such as dialectic defects or those established by bad habits become indelible in the adult."[30]

The importance of a good language environment for the infant becomes obvious:

Many of the defects which have become permanent in adults are due to *functional errors in the development* of the language during the period of infancy. If, for the attention which we pay to the correction of linguistic defects in children in the upper grades, we would substitute *a direction of the development* of the language while the child is still young, our results would be much more practical and valuable.[31]

Montessori recognizes that developmentally, the most important time of life is not that of university studies, but of so-called "preschool" learning from "birth to the age of six." This is the time when "intelligence itself . . . is being formed."[32] The child can absorb "much more culture at an early age than later," and "no amount of higher education can cancel what has been formed in infancy."[33]

The recognition of the crucial importance of the first years of life must be extended to the development of practical provision for fully utilizing this period. To cite but one example:

We have to conclude that scientific words are best taught to children between the ages of three and six, not in a mechanical way, of course, but in conjunction with the objects concerned, or in the course of their explorations. . .[34]

Montessori developed a vast array of programmed materials which indeed enable the child to learn basic vocabularies in geography, biology, geometry, etc.

Earlier, we stressed the fact that the child's sensitive periods are transitory. If, because adequate materials are not available or perhaps other conditions are unfulfilled, and the child is not able to work in accordance with the guidance of its sensitive period, the child "has lost its chance of a natural conquest, and has lost it forever."[35]

The child must have the materials with which to work. Montessori employed sandpaper letters, movable alphabets and other devices to enhance language development:

> The child, in looking at the letters, identifying them, and tracing them in the way they are written, is preparing himself both for reading and writing at the same time.[36]

Children can and will learn to write at four and read at five, but not if environmental shortcomings prevent them from doing so. Perhaps the major obstacle is adult misconception of the child's capacities:

> I believe that we must greatly modify our ideas regarding infant psychology, as soon as trained psychologists begin to observe the spontaneous manifestations of children, to the end of encouraging their tendencies.[37]

Never has objective observation by adults been needed more:

> No longer is it for the professor to apply psychology to childhood, but it is for the children themselves to reveal their psychology to those who study them.[38]

Montessori refers to the child as "an organism still in process of formation." The adult must understand that the child's rhythm of learning differs from the adult's:

> Children who are understanding something for the first time are extremely slow. Their life is governed in this respect by laws especially different from ours.[39]

A most important characteristic of the Montessori "prepared environment" is the opportunity it provides for the child to work at his own speed, repeating an activity until he has mastered it to his satisfaction. Montessori says: "The normal child always repeats the exercise with growing interest."[40] And finally, ". . . we must always remember that the child's sensitiveness is greater than anything we can imagine."[41]

SUMMARY

In this chapter, we have discussed briefly some selected Montessori contributions to the theory and practice of early childhood education, especially as they relate to language learning.

Montessori identified a number of sensitive periods—times of predisposition to particular learnings—in the child's mental development, such as a sensitive period for language, and another for order. During the former, for example, the child can learn language most readily.

Montessori wrote of the "Absorbent Mind" of the child—the mind able to absorb language and knowledge directly as the child engages in "auto-education." Because the child has this capacity for self-teaching, education can be conceived as a natural process which develops spontaneously in the human infant. Speaking as the harbinger of a revolution in education, Montessori described the role of the educator as one, not of teaching, but of helping the process of auto-education to expand by providing an environment to match the child's needs. This environment, for optimum language development, must feature programmed materials which afford every child the opportunity to learn exemplary speech, reading, and writing.[42]

REFERENCES

1. MONTESSORI, MARIA: *The Formation of Man.* Adyar, Madras 20, India, Theosophical Publishing House, 1955, p. 29.
2. _____: *Education for a New World.* Adyar, Madras 20, India, Kalakshetra Publications, Third Impress., 1959, p. 67.
3. _____: *The Child in the Church.* Edited by Mortimer Standing, London, Sands, 1929, p. 94.
4. *Ibid.,* p. 93.
5. MONTESSORI, MARIA: *The Discovery of the Child.* Translated by Mary Johnstone, Adyar, Madras 20, India, Kalakshetra Publications, Reprinted, 1958, p. 221.

6. _____: *The Secret of Childhood.* Translated and Edited by Barbara Carter, Bombay, Orient Longmans, New Impress., 1959, p. 63.
7. _____: *The Absorbent Mind.* Translated by Claude Claremont, Adyar, Madras 20, India, Theosophical Publishing House, 3rd Ed., 1961, p. 63.
8. _____: *The Formation of Man.* p. 118.
9. _____: *The Montessori Elementary Materials.* New York: Stokes, 1917, (Vol. II of *The Advanced Montessori Method),* p. 12.
10. _____: *The Absorbent Mind.* p. 106.
11. _____: *The Child in the Church.* p. 94.
12. _____: *The Secret of Childhood.* p. 54.
13. _____: *Spontaneous Activity in Education.* New York, Stokes, 1917, (Vol. I of *The Advanced Montessori Method),* p. 71.
14. _____: *The Child in the Church.* p. 84.
15. _____: *Spontaneous Activity in Education.* p. 109.
16. _____: *The Montessori Method.* New York, Stokes, 1912, p. 118.
17. _____: *Pedagogical Anthropology.* New York, Stokes, 1913, p. 443.
18. _____: *The Absorbent Mind.* pp. 23-24.
19. *Ibid.,* p. 24.
20. Montessori, Maria: *Reconstruction in Education.* Adyar, Madras 20, India, Theosophical Publishing House, 2nd Ed., 1948.
21. _____: *The Secret of Childhood.* p. 215.
22. _____: *The Absorbent Mind. p.* 66.
23. *Ibid.,* p. 67.
24. Montessori, Maria: *The Formation of Man.* p. 83.
25. _____: *The Secret of Childhood,* p. 73.
26. _____: *Pedagogical Anthropology.* p. 17.
27. _____: *The Absorbent Mind,* p. 27.
28. _____: *The Formation of Man,* p. 87.
29. _____: *Education for a New World.* p. 40.
30. _____: *The Montessori Method.* pp. 315-316.
31. *Ibid.,* p. 280.
32. Montessori, Maria: *The Absorbent Mind.* p. 21.
33. *Ibid.,* p. 181.
34. *Ibid.,* p. 174.
35. Montessori, Maria: *The Secret of Childhood.* p. 41.
36. _____: *The Montessori Elementary Material.* p. 443.
37. _____: *Pedagogical Anthropology.* p. 443.
38. _____: *The Absorbent Mind.* p. 3.
39. _____: *The Montessori Method.* p. 358.
40. *Ibid.,* p. 171.
41. Montessori, Maria: *The Absorbent Mind.* p. 132.
42. Orem, R.C. *A Montessori Handbook.* New York, Putnam, 1965, pp. 119-150. (Capricorn Edition, published 1966).

SUGGESTED READINGS, BRIEFLY ANNOTATED

1. FINN, J., and PERRIN, D.: *Teaching Machines and Programmed Learning: A Survey of the Industry, 1962.* U. S. Dept. of Health, Education, and Welfare, U.S. Office of Education. Washington, D.C., U.S. Government Printing Office, OE 34019, 1962.

Overview of the field, including illustrations of machines and a directory of programs.

2. FRANK, L.: Tactile communication. *Genetic Psychology Monographs, 56*:209-255, 1957.

A discussion of such areas as tactile experiences in personality development, cultural patterning of tactile experiences, and research possibilities.

3. FRY, E.: Programmed instruction in reading. *The Reading Teacher.* 453-459, 1964.

Programmed instructional materials, of varying quality and suitability, are rapidly becoming available in reading, including beginning reading.

4. GALANTER, EUGENE (ED): *Automatic Teaching: The State of the Art.* New York, Wiley, 1959.

Papers from the first conference on the Art and Science of the Automatic Teaching of Verbal and Symbolic Skills, on programming and programmers, teaching machines, etc.

5. GATES, A.: Controversies about teaching reading. *School and Society, 90,* 1962.

Possibilities of a Skinnerian approach to learning with programmed reading instruction are discussed.

6. LUMSDAINE, A.: Teaching machines and programmed learning. Washington, D.C., Department of Audio-Visual Instruction, National Education Association, 1960.

Some basic dimensions are briefly summarized.

7. MCNEIL, J., and KEISLER, E.: Value of the oral response in beginning reading: an experimental study using programmed instruction. *British Journal of Educational Psychology, 33*:p.162,1963.

The central concern of this study is the value of the oral response in early reading instruction. The subjects were 182 kindergarten children in California. The assumption is that five-year-olds can learn to read; the hypothesis is that programmed instruction allowing for oral responses will be more effective than the one that relies on "silent responses."

8. MONTESSORI, MARIA: *The Montessori Method.* New York, Stokes 1912.

Maria Montessori, M.D., was using "didactic materials" sixty years ago for the sensory, "motor" and intellectual education of three-to-six-year-olds. Some of this material stemmed from Seguin and other educators; much was developed by Montessori, her students, and teachers. It contains built-in "control of error," carefully arranged gradients of stimuli, and sequences of progressively more challenging tasks. Activity and movement are important in the Montessori system. There is frequent opportunity provided for "motor education" to develop manual skills and body coordination. Much use is made of the tactile sense. The child has freedom to choose his tasks and to proceed at his own pace in a "prepared environment" where the teacher serves as observer, exemplar, and guardian of the child's right to learn. Through preparation and practice the child develops self-confidence, inner discipline, and control of himself and of the environment. Allowed to concentrate on work of interest to himself, he observes, experiments, and creates. Learning becomes a process of making discoveries.

9. MORRILL, C.: Teaching machines: a review. *Psychological Bulletin, 58*: 1961.

Research is reviewed in terms of trends, problem areas, and problems of application.

10. OREM, R. C., (Ed.): *A Montessori Handbook.* New York, Putnam, 1965.

Doctor Montessori's own writings are interpreted in the light of recent developments in childhood learning and related fields, with contributions by nine experts in these fields.

11. OREM, R., and ALEXANDER, G.: What are the essential features of an effective Montessori school? *National Catholic Kindergarten Review,* Fall, 1965.

Guidelines relating to philosophy, personnel, physical plant, program, and pupils.

12. *Programs, '62: A Guide to Programmed Instructional Materials Available to Educators by September 1962.* Compiled and produced by Information Division, The Center for Programmed Instruction, Inc. and the U.S. Dept. of Health, Education, and Welfare, U.S. Office of Education. OE 34015. Washington, D.C., U.S. Gov. Print. Off., 1962.

A listing of 122 programs, with sample "frames."

13. SCHRAMM, W.: *The Newer Educational Media in the United States.* Paper prepared for the Meeting of Experts on the

Development and Use of New Methods and Techniques of Education, UNESCO House, Paris, March, 1962, Washington, D.C., U.S. National Commission for UNESCO.

The effectiveness of the newer educational media, as revealed by research, is discussed; includes bibliographies and notes on learning theory by Ernest Hilgard.

14. SKINNER, B. F.: Why we need teaching machines. *Cumulative Record,* New York, 1961.

B. F. Skinner, perhaps the major modern advocate of programmed learning and behaviorism, suggests that reading could be started in the nursery school with teaching machines.

Chapter Nine

RESEARCH AND EARLY READING*

MAIN POINTS

Two points of view regarding readiness:
   1. "The necessary mental age of 6½."
   2. The "meaninglessness of a specific mental age."

Many preschoolers have learned and are learning to read.

Limitations of the Morphett and Washburne-type studies.

Negative elements of the formal school situation for the young child.

Preschoolers of average intelligence can learn to read.

Many bright children are reading problems.

Children benefit from an early start in reading.

Preschoolers of lower IQ need early help in reading.

The similarity of learning to see and learning to hear words.

Problems in many public school classrooms stemming from:
   1. class size;
   2. class heterogeneity;
   3. uncertified teachers;
   4. teacher turnover;
   5. teacher training.

Other problems stemming from:
   1. reading needs of certain students neglected;
   2. interruptions;
   3. teachers' clerical duties;
   4. teachers' lack of understanding of research findings.

---

*Durkin, Dolores: Early readers—reflections after six years of research. *The Reading Teacher,* 18:3-7, 1964. "In 1957, when plans for my research were still somewhat vague and indefinite, the general response to the topic selected for study was an unenthusiastic response, to say the least. It was as if to think about the possibility of earlier reading instruction was to encourage a return to the era of child labor abuses." p. 3.

IN REVIEWING THE CURRENT EDUCATIONAL and psychological literature dealing with early reading experience, one encounters two contradictory points of view. Many reading authorities recommend that, for best results, formal reading instruction for children should not begin before they attain a mental age of at least six or six and one-half.

Harrison, studying those factors which might predict reading success, concluded that a mental age of six and one-half on both the Detroit and Binet tests was most conducive to reading growth. According to Harrison ". . . it is safe to state that a mental age of at least six years must be reached before success will be probable, and we can be much more certain of success if the mental age is six years and six months."[1] In the same vein, Morphett and Washburne, after studying 141 first-grade children concluded that ". . . the percentage of children who learned to read satisfactorily is greatest at the mental ages of six years and six months, and of seven years." They assert, therefore, that ". . . it seems safe to state that, by postponing the teaching of reading until children reach a mental level of six and a half years, teachers can greatly decrease the chances of failure and discouragement and can correspondingly increase their efficiency."[2]

It follows from this point of view, then, that the child of average IQ ($IQ = \frac{\text{Mental Age}}{\text{Chronological Age}} \times 100$) should not be introduced to reading until he has reached a chronological age of six and one-half, or even seven. And the child of below average IQ should have reading instruction delayed even longer.

Reading introduced too early—before the child is ready to learn—before he has sufficient mental maturity—will cause reading failure, according to the readiness proponents.

On the other hand, a number of investigators have reached conclusions which are at variance with the concept of "six and one-half as the minimum mental age for beginning reading." Gates and Bond, for example, studied children entering Grade One with mental ages ranging from four years and eleven months to seven years and eight months. When they related the mental ages to reading achievement, no crucial or initial point above which very few fail and below which a large proportion fail was apparent.[3] Gates has concluded that ". . . statements concerning the necessary mental age at which a pupil can be expected to learn to read are essentially meaningless."[4] Davidson worked for four and one-half months with three small groups of preschool children: a bright three-, a normal four-, and a dull five-year-old group. All had mental ages of approximately four years. After the relatively brief instruction (the highest number of reading lessons received by any one subject was sixty-one), the number of words recognized out of context by the thirteen individual subjects ranged from 20 to 269 words.

The most successful subject was the youngest one, having been tested two days after her third birthday. A year later, this girl was reading from a Fourth Reader.[5]

We have then, on the face of it, two positions which would appear to be mutually exclusive. Yet, for reasons very similar to those underlying the phonics-sight recognition controversy, we believe that the contradiction can be resolved.

Those opposed to early reading experience for the child have tended to base their opposition on the results of studies and investigations made in the primary grades. Several investigators, for example, have charted the progress made in reading, and other school subjects, by students who started formal schooling before attaining a mental age of six and those who started after that age mentally. In general, after several years, it was discovered that the older students mentally had made at least as much if not more progress, and effected a better adjustment to the school situation than did the younger students.[6]

These studies seemed to indicate that children who start school before six may have greater difficulty learning to read and are generally more prone to develop psychological problems in the traditional school situation.[7]

One of the most influential studies, by Morphett and Washburne,[8] was the already-mentioned one in 1931 in Winnetka, Illinois. This study involved 141 students entering the first grade. They were given an IQ test to determine mental age, and their progress was charted through the first grade. The results indicated that success in reading increased up to the mental age of six and one-half, clearly suggesting that the older students learned better than did the younger. This study led many teachers to believe that reading instruction should be postponed until six or later. One writer, Edgar A. Doll,[9] has gone so far as to suggest that reading instruction should be delayed until the third grade.

In 1955, Inez King[10] studied two groups of fifty children starting school. One group started before the age of six, and the other after that age. Again, the younger students, after six years of school, had made significantly less progress than the students who started after six. King noted that the younger students had more adjustmental problems. Clyde Baer,[11] in a similar study which matched two groups of intellectually superior children, found higher grades and achievement in the older group and better emotional adjustment. It is important to note that many of these studies dealing with academic achievement of the young child in the school situation uncovered some adjustmental problems.

The adjustment factor in reading appears even more important in studies of students with reading disability. Many writers who have investigated the causes of reading disability have found that early school experience appeared to have had an adverse effect on these children. Ruth Strang[12] and others have pointed out that once a child has failed to cope with a subject, the subject becomes psychologically charged with negative associations and the child builds up blocks and resists further instruction. Bond and Tinker have described such a situation:

> He gets farther and farther behind as time goes by. Inability to cope with the assignments produces frustration which leads to feelings of inadequacy, inferiority, insecurity, and perhaps even rebellion. Such a child is likely to develop an attitude of indifference to reading. He may even come to hate reading and all persons and activities connected with reading activities.[13]

In general, it has been noted that the very young student who gets off to a bad start will tend to have problems throughout his school career; but one must observe that this research, while purportedly discussing reading, is actually considering two interrelated factors: reading achievement and school adjustment. There is strong evidence that the child under six is not ready for the formal school situation (at least as it exists in our typical schools). But when the educational theorists identify starting school with learning to read, they are confusing intellectual and adjustmental aspects of human development. After all, many children learn to read outside of school and some children go to school without learning to read. Though, obviously, starting school and learning to read are often concurrent experiences, they are in many respects quite distinct. Beginning school is in large part a psychological and social process through which the child learns to adjust to restrictions on his movements and attention, and to new demands on his personality and social skills. Learning to read, on the other hand, is essentially a perceptual-cognitive task.

Those studies which are frequently cited to support the popular notion that early reading is detrimental are suspect on two grounds. First, they fail to distinguish between the intellectual process of learning to read and the psychological process of adjusting to school. Second, as studies of reading progress, they are faulty in design, as they lack adequate controls. The fact that children under five tend to have more difficulty learning to read in the first grade may mean that they are not ready to learn, but it might also mean that the system of instruction is faulty or that the child's emotional immaturity is creating anxiety which is in turn blocking his efforts to learn. As designed and interpreted, these studies of early reading mask these important variables, and must be limited in implication to a simple statement of their results: children who start school before six may have more psychological problems and make poorer academic progress on the average than older starting students.

Inferences drawn from such studies as that by Morphett and Washburne about reading readiness are very doubtful at best.[14] In fact, such studies may be more indicative of the inadequacies of elementary school reading instruction than of the limitations of the child as a learner.[15] Gates notes that the difficulties involved in teaching reading to a large class are so great that the average child learns rather slowly. But when we look at the records of children who learned to read *before* they went to school, we find that they are, subsequently, among the most successful students. Many of these children who learn to read by themselves or under the casual direction of older siblings or interested adults have mastered the art of reading before the age of five and some even before the age of four.[17,18,19,20]

We have here a natural control group for the educator who theorizes about the difficulties attending early reading experience in school. We have here very young children being exposed to reading in a home environment without the complicating psychological factor of school adjustment. In a number of studies and investigations of the preschool reader it has been found that, in an informal or home environment, children can learn to read.[21] These reports of the success of early reading instruction, however informal, outside of the school situation, when contrasted with the studies of early reading difficulty in the school situation naturally suggest a question. Is it the child's lack of readiness or the stress of adjusting to the school environment which is at fault?

There is little doubt that the complex nature of new social relationships, the rigid organization of the classroom, and the formal structure of teacher presentation places great demands on the very young child. It may well be that children under six are inadequate psychologically to the task of adjustment and *as a consequence* may have learning problems. But to reach conclusions about the nature of language development in the child on the basis of early school performance is to confuse two separate dimensions of human development. Because the child is not ready for the usual school format does not mean that he is not ready for exposure to reading,[22] for, as we have suggested, wherever very young normal children have been exposed to reading in a preschool situation, they have made some progress.

Nor is it true that these early readers in a home environment were all unusually intelligent and therefore gifted with special learning talents. In one study, one-third of the children who learned to read before school had IQ's of 110 or less.[23] Of course, many of the children who teach themselves to read are very bright, but on the other hand, children of normal intelligence have learned to read before school. Moreover, many bright children have trouble learning to read and some of them subsequently become reading problems.

Witty and Kopel have reported that 90 per cent of poor

readers of both elementary and high-school ages have IQ's from 80 to 110 with about equal numbers between 80 and 90, 90 and 100, and 100 and 110. They conclude that ". . . most poor readers have sufficient mental ability to read satisfactorily . . ."[24] Robinson reports that ". . . severely retarded readers may be found with low, average, and superior intelligence." Individuals in the latter group may have IQ's as high as 150.[25]

Intelligence, while of some import, does not appear to be the key factor in learning to read, any more than it is the key factor in learning to talk.

Some insight into why certain children master reading before school has been suggested by the work of Dolores Durkin, a reading specialist who has been doing research in early reading since 1957. She has discovered that children learn to read not because of parental pressure or high intelligence but largely because these children are raised in an environment where the adults are very interested in reading and the child is given extensive opportunity to learn to read. Another reading teacher, Walter B. Barbe of the Reading Center at the University of Chattanooga made the same observation:

> Another amazing thing about interest is that the more interest the teacher and the parents have in reading, the more easily interest is developed in the child. There are many teachers who actually never do any formal teachings of reading and yet many of their children learn to read.[26]

In 1962, **Durkin** published the results of a study which have revolutionary implications for the teaching of reading.[27] In this carefully designed study, **Doctor Durkin** followed the academic progress of fifty children who had been taught to read at home. The preschool readers were tested before starting school and carefully matched with a control group of similar mental potentials for purposes of comparison. The students were followed for a period of three years, and the results of the study are most significant. The early readers made an excellent adjustment to school, and none of the group had any problem in learning to extend their reading skill in the school situation. In fact their progress in reading was greater than would have been predicted on the basis of preschool intelligence tests.

When these predicted scores were calculated, it was found that for all the children who were early readers actual scores in reading were greater than would have been predicted for them on the basis of their intelligence.[28]

The intelligence of the group is also worth noting, for in contrast to the popular notion that all preschool readers are in the "gifted" category, many of this group were in the normal range of intelligence. Moreover, Doctor Durkin notes:

> Two observations can be made concerning these fifteen early readers who had intelligence quotients of 120 or less. First, they appear to have profited from their early start. Second, the lower the child's intelligence quotient, the greater seems to be the advantage of starting early.[29]

Interestingly enough, the study was handicapped by the fact that about 25 per cent of the early readers were double promoted in the first two years and were not available for matching with the control group at the end of the third grade.

Doctor Durkin's conclusions are worth quoting at some length.

> ... educators have been encouraging parents, perhaps unintentionally, to put a child's questions about words into a do-not-touch category on the assumption that what a child learns about reading before he enters school interferes with subsequent school instruction. This study of early readers does not verify this assumption. In fact, what is tentatively suggested is that children of relatively lower intelligence especially benefit from an early start. Should this finding be duplicated in a second study recently begun in another school system, it would mean that slower children need contact with learning to read that is spread out over time. Instead of a postponement of reading instruction, they need an earlier start with it.[30]

Doctor Durkin's second longitudinal study of early readers, "Children Who Read Before Grade I: A Second Study" supports the foregoing conclusions. Apparently, no school problems are encountered when children get initial help with reading during their preschool years.

Normal preschool children, then, can learn to read with no detrimental side effects; and the oft-repeated message warning parents not to teach their children to read before school is based on research which actually measured the learning problems of immature students who had difficulty adjusting to school, rather than the normal child's native capacity to learn. The authors, in reviewing all available research on early or preschool reading experience, have been able to find no evidence that preschool exposure to reading will hinder a child's progress in school; this view passed on to parents by well-intentioned teachers has little support in the research. Durkin, one of the few educational theorists who has studied reading in the preschool child, comments:

> Briefly, this message is to warn these parents not to teach preschool children to read on the assumption that what a child learns about reading before he gets to school interferes with subsequent school instruction. I have no idea how this rumor got started.[31]

There is, then, no contradiction between the high academic achievement of preschool readers and the poor showing of children who start school before six. The first demonstrates the value of early stimulation for the child's general intellectual development; and the second suggests that with our present educational methods we cannot introduce very young children into a traditional learning situation without a certain percentage developing learning problems.

The skill and speed with which all normal children, regardless of IQ, learn to speak, demonstrates the child's ability to learn language. The real matter at issue is the best time and methods to teach them. As has been pointed out, some studies have indicated that the very young child does not learn well in the school situation, and yet much evidence exists to prove that it is only the very young child who has any real aptitude for language, visual or aural. Certainly, during the very period in which educational theorists maintain that the child cannot learn visual language readily, the same child is mastering spoken language easily and naturally.

The normal child is inquisitive and open to experience and new ideas. He has great natural curiosity and intellectual energy. Any parent or interested adult who has tried to cope with the incessant questions of the average four-year-old can attest the truth of this statement. Before going to school, all normal children evince a great interest in learning about their world, but after only a few months of school experience, many have lost interest and are even hostile towards the formal learning situation. How this intellectual curiosity becomes transformed into apathy and failure is a question that perhaps more educators should examine.

Arthur and Carolyn Staats, at Arizona State University, have been investigating the development of speech and reading behavior in the very young child. They have concluded that learning to read is very similar to mastering speech, and they raise the question: Why should speech be mastered so easily and universally and reading instruction be relatively more difficult and less successful? They note that it has been common to find fault with some aspect of the child as a learner:

> It is commonly suggested that such uneven development is a result of some biological defect, such as neurological impairment. However unless there is some independent observation of a defect, this type of conclusion may simply be ad hoc. If the child is capable of acquiring differential speech response to the ordinary visual stimuli in a normal manner, then it should be possible for visual stimuli also to come to control the verbal responses. There is certainly no obvious difference in the stimuli themselves, since both are visual and both are complex. Ordinary language behavior requires that verbal responses be under the control of subtle aspects of one's stimulus environment. The same thing is true of reading, i.e., the stimuli are no more complex.[32]

In other words, as has been stressed throughout this book, since learning to see words is closely parallel to learning to hear words, the relatively greater difficulty we have in teaching reading must stem from our methods of exposure and quality of instruction rather than from any limitation in the child as a learner.

When confronted with learning problems, some educators have tended to find fault with the child's home environment, his intelligence, emotional maturity, or reading readiness. However, a careful look at the conditions under which most children are introduced to reading suggests quite another explanation.

Throughout this book the authors have maintained that it is imperative that every parent give serious consideration to the merits of teaching his own child the fundamentals of reading. Primarily, the preschool period is the naturally absorptive period when the child will learn most easily and efficiently. In addition, there are many secondary factors in the typical public school classroom which may actually retard reading development.

Let us examine a few of these factors.

There is the problem of class size. Although the average elementary class in this country contains approximately thirty students[33] a figure far too high for effective instruction at this level, many teachers are actually straining under a burden of forty or more pupils. Even with this overcrowding, not all children can be squeezed in for a full school day. As a matter of fact, during the fall of 1961, approximately one-third million elementary pupils attended school for less than a regular school day because of classroom and other shortages.[34]

There is the problem of heterogeneity within the classroom. At any level of instruction, there will be a reading ability range from five to seven grades within the same class.[35] This means that, in a third grade class, some students will be reading at the first grade level or below while a few are at the sixth grade level or above in this skill.

There is the problem of uncertified teachers. In the fall of 1961, 65,000 *full-time* persons holding substandard certificates were "teaching" in elementary classrooms. That is, these provisional teachers lacked the academic preparation necessary for the lowest regular teaching certificate in the state where employed. It should be pointed out that in many states this requirement is *less than* a bachelor's degree. Also, the above figure does not include unqualified part-time or substitute teachers.[36] Stated in another way, more than one and one-third million elementary pupils during this time were taught by unqualified teachers.

We stress the fact that these statistics apply to the grade school years, the time when, theoretically, the learning sets for the basic tool subjects such as reading are supposed to be established.

Teacher turnover is a grave problem. It continues at the rate of 10 per cent. That is, one in ten public school teachers leaves his job every year. A *Life* article noted that 1962-63 was to be the last year in the profession for approximately 125,000 public school teachers. And a substantial proportion of those who left are among the *best teachers*.[37]

It has been estimated that a million and one-half persons have been "in and out" of the teaching profession since the outbreak of World War II. Some schools lose 25 per cent of their teachers annually.

How many first-graders have a change in teachers during this crucial first year? No one knows.

Moreover, there is the problem of teacher training. To be more exact, the problem is one of lack of teacher training. The Harvard-Carnegie Reading Study,[38] which involved a nationwide survey of hundreds of institutions preparing tomorrow's teachers of reading, presents a dismal picture. In the report of findings, we note that college students who major in education rank in academic ability below those in other departments. There is poor screening of applicants in teacher training programs. The typical education student graduates with only a "general concept" of the retarded reader. The most mature features of the reading process appear to be "seriously neglected." Too little time, in other words, is given to instructional techniques in the teaching of reading.

One study indicates that only two of three persons trained for the teaching profession enter the field in the first place and of these, perhaps 10 per cent stay as long as ten years.[39] The average teaching career is about five years. Many young persons "try teaching" for a year or two, then leave for marriage or other reasons. Unfortunately for the pupils, it is generally recognized that a beginning teacher needs several years of experience before he can begin to approach maximum efficiency. The havoc that conditions such as these wreak on children struggling to learn to read can only be imagined. Kottmeyer, assistant superintendent of instruction for the St. Louis, Missouri public schools, wrote in 1959:

> The plain fact of the matter is that poor teaching or poor learning conditions are probably responsible for more reading disability than all the other investigated causes put together.[40]

Then there are other problems which the parent may wish to consider. Recent criticisms of public education, many of them made by teachers, include the following:

1. The reading needs of superior students are seriously neglected. These readers are often left virtually "on their own."[41]
2. The unjustified interruptions during the reading periods in school may well account, according to at least one authority, for many children failing to learn to read.[42]
3. The reading teachers' time is sapped by clerical, noninstructional chores.[43]
4. Teachers are handicapped by inadequate understanding of research in reading. If they are aware of current findings, they often fail to apply them.[44]

Much of what passes for "reading instruction" in many American schools is inadequate and perhaps, in some instances, damaging. Results of studies which indicate that children under six have difficulty in learning under such circumstances are really to be expected. The only errors that have been made with such studies have been errors of interpretation. For it is not that the five-year-old cannot learn, or is not "ready to read," but rather it is true that our schools are not yet equipped in theory or practice to teach reading to the very young child.

SUMMARY

A number of reading authorities have discouraged early reading, and advised parents to adopt a "hands-off" policy regarding teaching their preschoolers to read. However, the studies that are frequently cited to support such a policy provide little or no evidence that reading instruction should be postponed. These studies confuse the perceptual-cognitive task of learning to read with the psychological process of adjusting to school, and indirectly show many of the limitations for the young learner of the usual school situation.

The work of a number of investigators, but principally Dolores Durkin, indicates that young children of varied IQ's can learn to read with parental assistance. Early readers adjust satisfactorily to school and their early reading experience is reflected in their progress in reading.

There are many factors in the typical public school classroom which may affect the learning of reading unfavorably.

REFERENCES

1. HARRISON, M. LUCILLE: *Reading Readiness*. Boston, Houghton Mifflin, p. 8, 1936.
2. MORPHETT, MABEL, and WASHBURNE, CARLETON: When should children begin to read? *Elementary School Journal, 31*:503, 1931.
3. GATES, ARTHUR, and BOND, GUY: Reading readiness: a study of factors determining success and failure in beginning reading. *Teachers College Record, 37*:680, 1936.
4. GATES, ARTHUR: The necessary mental age for beginning reading. *Research in the Three R's*, Ed. by Hunnicutt, C.W., and Iverson, W., New York, Harper, p. 62, 1958.
5. DAVIDSON, HELEN: An experimental study of bright, average, and dull children at the four-year mental level. *Genetic Psychology Monographs, 9*:119-289, 1931.
6. THOMSON, JENNIE: Big gains from postponed reading. *Journal of Education, 118*:445-446, 1934.
7. WITTY, PAUL, and KOPEL, DAVID: Preventing reading disability: the reading readiness factor. *Educational Administration and Supervision: Including Teacher Training, 22*:401-418, 1936.
8. MORPHETT, MABEL, and WASHBURNE, CARLETON: *op. cit.*, 496-503.
9. DOLL, EDGAR: Varieties of slow learners. *Exceptional Children, 20*:61-64, 1953.
10. KING, INEZ: Effect of age of entrance into grade I upon achievement in elementary school. *Elementary School Journal, 55*:331-336, 1955.
11. BAER, CLYDE: The school progress and adjustment of underage and overage students. *Journal of Educational Psychology, 49*:17-19, 1958.
12. STRANG, RUTH, and BRACKEN, DOROTHY: *Making Better Readers*. Boston, Heath, p. 7, 1957.
13. BOND, GUY, and TINKER, MILES: *Reading Difficulties: Their Diagnosis and Correction*. New York, Appleton-Century-Crofts, p. 115, 1957.
14. MCCRACKEN, GLENN: Have we overemphasized the readiness factor? *Elementary English, 29*:271-276, 1952.
15. GATES, ARTHUR, and BOND, GUY: Reading readiness: a study of factors determining success and failure in beginning reading. *Teachers College Record, 37*:679-685, 1936.
16. GATES, ARTHUR: Unsolved problems in reading: a symposium. *Elementary English*, 331-334, 1954
17. MONEY, JOHN, (ED.): *Reading Disability: Progress and Research Needs in Dyslexia*. Baltimore, Johns Hopkins Press. See "Case No. 2," p. 26, 1962.
18. DURKIN, DOLORES: Reading instruction and the five-year-old child.

Challenge and Experiment in Reading. International Reading Association Conference Proceedings, 7, 1962, New York, Scholastic Magazines. pp. 23-27.
19. ANDERSON, IRVING, and DEARBORN, WALTER: *The Psychology of Teaching Reading.* New York, Ronald, 1952, See The concept of reading readiness, Chapter 2.
20. STRANG, RUTH: Reading: a panel discussion. Chap. 17 in *Promoting Maximal Reading Growth Among Able Learners.* Robinson, Helen, Ed., Chicago, University of Chicago Press, pp. 183-185, 1954.
21. FOWLER, WILLIAM: Cognitive learning in infancy and early childhood. *Psychological Bulletin,* 59:116-152, 1962. See pp. 121-128.
22. DURRELL, DONALD: *Improving Reading Instruction,* Yonkers-on-Hudson, New York, World Book, 1956. Erroneous Concepts of Reading Readiness, pp. 46-48.
23. DURKIN, DOLORES: *Op. cit.,* p. 24.
24. WITTY, PAUL, and KOPEL, DAVID: *Reading and the Educative Process.* Boston, Ginn, p. 228, 1939.
25. ROBINSON, HELEN: *Why Pupils Fail in Reading.* Chicago, University of Chicago Press, p. 67, 1946.
26. BARBE, WALTER: Why children have trouble in reading. *Education,* 78:521, 1958.
27. DURKIN, DOLORES: An earlier start in reading? *The Elementary School Journal,* 63:146-151, 1962.
28. *Ibid.,* p. 149.
29. *Ibid.,* p. 149.
30. *Ibid.,* p. 150.
31. DURKIN, DOLORES: *Op. Cit.,* p. 23.
32. STAATS, ARTHUR, and STAATS, CAROLYN: A comparison of the development of speech and reading behavior with implications for research. *Child Development,* 33:831-846, 1962.
33. SCHLOSS, SAMUEL, and HOBSON, CAROL: *Fall 1961 Statistics on Enrollment, Teachers, and Schoolhousing in Full-Time Public Elementary and Secondary Day Schools.* Circular No. 676. U.S. Department of Health, Education and Welfare, U.S. Gov. Print. Off., p. 2, 1962.
34. *Ibid.,* p. 3.
35. DOLCH, EDWARD A.: *A Manual for Remedial Reading.* 2nd Ed. Champaign, Ill., Garrard Press, p. 1, 1957.
36. SCHLOSS, SAMUEL, and HOBSON, CAROL: *Op. Cit.,* p. 2.
37. MERYMAN, RICHARD: How we drive teachers to quit. *Life,* 53:104ff, 1962.
38. AUSTIN, MARY: *The Torch Lighters: Tomorrow's Teachers of Reading.* Cambridge, Mass., Harvard University Graduate School of Education. Distributed by Harvard University Press, 1961. See especially Chap. 8, Recommendations, pp. 139-157.

39. Keeping abreast in research. *Phi Delta Kappan, 44*:127, 1962.
40. KOTTMEYER, WILLIAM: *Teacher's Guide for Remedial Reading.* St. Louis, Webster Publishing Co., p. 16, 1959.
41. ABRAHAM, WILLARD: *A New Look at Reading: A Guide to the Language Arts.* Boston, Porter Sargent Publisher, p. 11, 1956.
42. BARBE, WALTER: Instructional causes of poor reading. *Education, 77*: 534-540, 1957.
43. MCCRACKEN, GLENN: *The Right to Learn.* Chicago, Regnery, 1959.
44. AUSTIN, MARY: *Op. Cit.,* pp. 61, 149.

ADDITIONAL READINGS

1. DAWE, H.: A study of the effect of an educational program upon language development and related mental functions in young children. *Journal of Experimental Education, 11*:200-209, 1942.
2. DURRELL, D.: Preschool and kindergarten experience. *Development in and Through Reading: The 60th Yearbook of the National Society for the Study of Education, Part I.* Chicago, University of Chicago Press, p. 257, 1961.
3. FAST, I: Kindergarten training and grade I reading. *Journal of Educational Psychology, 48*:52-57, 1957.
4. GUNDERSON, D.: *Research in Reading Readiness.* Bulletin No. 8. U.S. Department of Health, Education and Welfare, Washington, D.C., U.S. Gov. Print. Off., 1964.
5. GUNDERSON, D.: *Research in Reading at the Primary Level: An Annotated Bibliography,* U.S. Department of Health, Education, and Welfare, Washington, D.C., U.S. Gov. Print. Off., 1963.
6. HAEFNER, RALPH: The influence of the typewriter on reading in the elementary school. *Elementary English Review, 13*:291-94, 1936.
7. HEWITT, F.: Teaching reading to an autistic boy through operant conditioning. *The Reading Teacher,* 613-618, 1964.
8. HORN, E.: A child's early experiences with the letter A. *Journal of Educational Psychology, 20*:161-68, 1929.
9. KEISTER, B.: Reading skills acquired by five-year-old children. *Elementary School Journal, 41*:587-96, 1941.
10. KELLEY, M.L.: When are children "ready" to read? *Saturday Review,* July 20, 1963, pp. 58-59ff.
11. PECK, L., and WALLING, R.: A preliminary study of the eidetic imagery of preschool children. *Journal of Genetic Psychology, 47*:168-192, 1935.
12. PURDY, D.M.: Eidetic images and plasticity of perception. *Journal of Genetic Psychology 15*:437-454, 1936.
13. RAMBUSCH, N.: At what age should systematic reading instruction begin? *Reading as an Intellectual Activity: International Reading Association Conference Proceedings. 8:* 1963.
14. SHELDON, W.: President's report. *The Reading Teacher,* 287, 1962.

15. _____, Teaching the very young to read. *The Reading Teacher,* *16*:163-169, 1962.
16. _____, Should the very young be taught to read? *NEA Journal,* *52*:20-22, 1963.
17. SMITH, N.B.: Readiness for reading, *Elementary English, 27*:91-106, 1950.
18. WITTY, P.: A balanced reading program for the gifted. *The Reading Teacher, 16*: 1963.

Chapter Ten

SOME ADVANTAGES OF PRESCHOOL READING

MAIN POINTS

Assumption that preschoolers cannot learn to read.
Evidence that preschoolers can learn to read.
Various methods of teaching early reading successful.
Children learning to read by TV.
Young child's unique capacity for learning to read "naturally."
Utilizing this capacity by exposing child to visual language.
Preschool readers have wide range of intelligence.
The non-reader, not the early reader, is the school problem.
Evidence of early reading in superior readers.
Importance of home environment in stimulating preschool reading.
High native intelligence wasted in inadequate environment.
Delaying of teaching of reading a major factor in reading problems.

HISTORICALLY, parents, educators and society at large have assumed that very young children generally could not learn to read. Those cases of preschoolers who did, indeed, learn to read have often been explained away by reference to "precociousness" on the part of children, or "pushing" on the part of parents. We have, without adequately examining the matter, tended to regard reading as too difficult a skill to be acquired by the average child during his preschool years. Interestingly enough, during this preschool period, all normal children are able to master one or more spoken languages. But we have given as little thought to the miracle of a child's mastery of speech as we have to the assumption that he cannot learn to read. We take for granted that the five-year-old will have learned to speak but not to read.

But, upon careful investigation, we find that there is overwhelming evidence, both scientific and informal, both historical and contemporary, that children can learn to read before the age at which they traditionally start to school. First of all, there are to be found hundreds of references to early reading scattered in general works. Letters, diaries, biographies, and histories have all reported instances of children under five—even under four—learning to read.

More formally there have been dozens of documented investigations, especially in recent years, by educators, psychologists, and other behavioral scientists concerned with the phenomenon of preschool reading. A number of these have been formal research projects with experimental designs, making objective evaluation possible, and they have been reported in scientific journals.

These reports of early reading discuss many kinds of children, including those of superior, average, and even below average intelligence. Many methods and techniques of instruction are reported: phonics, sight recognition, sandpaper letters, "talking typewriters," etc.

It is interesting to observe that these investigators, working with children of varied age and intelligence, and employing a range of equipment and procedures, have all experienced a considerable degree of success in teaching preschoolers to read.

Today there are a number of active and successful programs of early reading instruction for children being conducted by universities, school systems and other institutions throughout the United States. At the same time, hundreds of infant schools around the world patterned on Montessori principles are teaching their pupils to read.

One of the most striking demonstrations of the child's capacity for early reading has occurred through exposure of our children to television. Since the advent of the "TV in every living room," uncounted numbers of children are being helped to learn to read to some extent before they enter school. As a first step, they are learning to recognize the commercial names and symbols of advertised products. The designers of advertisements, with an excellent grasp of learning psychology, make the names large and clear, associate them with objects and products, and repeat them, often with attention-holding tunes and cartoons.

ADVANTAGES OF PRESCHOOL READING

Recently, a number of educators and behavioral scientists have initiated programs to study systematically the potential of television for teaching reading. If very young children can learn some words incidentally from TV commercials, what might they learn from carefully designed programs aimed specifically at reading? These television programs are already showing that adults have literally prevented children from learning to read by keeping reading a secret.[1] By making the words very small and crowding them together on a page so that the child cannot comprehend what they refer to, we have made the printed word comparatively inaccessible to the child's eyes and brain. The child can only learn in a situation in which his brain gets a sufficiently clear signal or stimulus from the environment. It is not that children cannot learn to read; rather, they have been denied the opportunity to learn! Children lack the visual skills necessary to cope with the small words of books designed for the mature reader. Also, because of the format, children cannot perceive the relationship between the words and their referents. If adults whispered all their spoken communications, children would not learn to talk either. In a sense, normal type size for adults is "whispered" writing for children.

When normal preschool children are exposed to large clear words which are plainly associated with objects, actions, or persons, they learn to read the words. The question is not whether such children can learn to read, but what they will learn to read. Will it be the slogans of the advertiser or the basic expressions of our language heritage?

Not only do we have evidence that young children can learn to read, but we also have very strong indications that only very young children can acquire reading directly and naturally from the environment.[2] This latter point is worth some review.

They have a special aptitude for language learning. We have long recognized this in relation to *spoken* language, but we have missed the obvious fact that it must also apply to *visual* language. Children of all nations and cultures master the language or languages of their environment with no formal instruction and frequently with little adult cooperation.

The adult brain never equals the child's in this respect, and the adult is rarely if ever as comfortable in a second language as he is in his native tongue. At this moment, there are thousands of young adults of normal intelligence in high school and college striving to learn a second language. How many of them will truly master this language? In point of fact, few of them will learn much more than a limited vocabulary and grammar. At the same time infants throughout the world are learning to speak the same languages with no help from a professional adult. This is possible because the young child has a special sensitivity to certain kinds of experience, including language. We have always recognized this at a popular level, and every society displays some understanding of the child as being "very impressionable." The child's mind is in a formative condition and early influences tend to be permanent.[3] The sounds and sights of childhood are most influential in determining the character of the adult personality. The adult resists basic change and no matter how long a time an adult may spend in another culture or country he will tend to reflect in attitude, mannerism, and preference, the country of his origin.

Students of language have known for some time that language is most readily acquired at an early age. Children who have had restricted language experience in childhood are likely as adults to be limited in speech and even intelligence.[4] In fact, young children who have received no exposure to language in their formative years may be unable to develop speech to any extent.

The natural time to introduce the basic forms of language is early childhood, and later it will be difficult for the brain to think and speak in any but its native tongue or tongues. We have been misled in limiting the child's language exposure to speech. We have not realized that if the child's brain can learn symbols through the sense of *hearing,* it could do the same through the sense of *sight.* After all, it is the brain that learns language, not the ears or eyes.[5] The ear has no aptitude for speech, nor the eye for reading. It is the human brain that is capable of processing symbols. Many animals have better sight or better hearing, or both, than do human beings, but they do not have the capacity to develop an abstract symbolic language. This language faculty of man is a part of his general intelligence and is only incidentally related to the senses through which he receives and expresses language forms.

If the brain can learn language through the ears it could in a parallel way master language through the eyes. And if, as we have pointed out, there is a sensitive period when the brain is most receptive to basic language forms then this sensitivity must also be a central process of human intelligence. If adults cannot learn a second language without retaining some accent of their native tongue then it is the brain not the ear drum (or some such external organ) which is responsible. So the language aptitude of the young child is really a transitory condition of the central nervous system which applies to all forms of language—written or spoken.

If the majority of children do not learn to read the "natural way," the way they learn to talk, it can only be that they are not being allowed to learn to read thus. They are not being exposed to the graphic symbols of reading as they are to auditory symbols of speech.

The fact that normal children recognize signs and television slogans proves that they can read words when given an opportunity. The success of past and present reading programs for very young children provides additional evidence of the child's capacity for early reading.

If adults would label some of the child's world with appropriate visual symbols, as we do now with aural symbols, and if adults would make large-lettered words easily accessible and relate them to objects in the child's environment, then children would begin to read just as naturally as they begin to talk.

By delaying the child's exposure to printed language we are in effect helping to create the millions of reading problems that now plague our schools. Some authorities estimate that as many as 30 per cent of our normal students have serious reading problems. Thirty per cent of a population having difficulty with a basic language art would seem to indicate that our method of instruction must be at fault. For these normal children have not had any significant problems in mastering spoken language. By denying the child extensive exposure to visual language forms during his formative period we are in effect forcing him to master reading as an adult masters a foreign language.

As a consequence of this practice, he will likely always be less comfortable with reading than with speech. Most adults, for example, read virtually as they talk. They subvocalize each word, thus translating the "foreign language" of visual forms into the "native tongue" of spoken language.

There is no reason why we should not read as spontaneously and as naturally as we talk.

If a complex sensory-motor behavior pattern is to be integrated into the central nervous system, so that it functions spontaneously and unconsciously, it must be introduced before the age of six. This applies to swimming, music, walking, talking, and reading.

As we noted earlier, there have been numerous instances of preschool reading which have been observed and reported by competent persons. Some of these reports date back a half-century or more, but it has only been in the past several years that preschool reading has emerged as a field in its own right. The next decade will undoubtedly see a continued expansion of research into the many interesting implications of early reading.

Although many of the early readers who have been reported to date were in one sense or another gifted, enough cases of children with average intelligence and even below average intelligence have been reported to prove that superior intelligence by itself is not enough to account for the performance of these readers.

The advantage that accrues to the early reader whether he be gifted or not is manifest. Even though there is still prevalent in some quarters a notion to the effect that preschool reading can interfere with the child's school adjustment, as we have noted, research does not support such a notion.

But even if the research on early learning were more ambiguous, common sense would indicate that being able to read to some extent would be of great value to any child starting school (unless, of course, the teacher resented this achievement and discriminated against the early reader.) Why does the reading child hold a great advantage over his struggling peers? At the very outset, he is likely to become a center of favorable attention, and while others may have to work hard to learn, his school experience should be more pleasant if not easy. Whatever some persons may say about the "dangers" of early reading, they will find it difficult not to admit that it is the non-reader or poor reader who is the problem. It is certainly not the child who reads easily and well who suffers in school, but the unfortunate student who cannot seem to make sense out of the printed words that constitute the path to learning. Academic deficiencies stem more frequently from "failure" to read well, than from "ability to read."

An ever-greater number of studies are demonstrating the advantages of early reading. One of the most convincing of these studies was made by Lawrence M. Kasdon. While completing his doctoral dissertation at Stanford University, Kasdon studied the early reading backgrounds of fifty superior readers.[6] These readers, from nine colleges in the metropolitan Los Angeles area, ranked highest on a reading test administered to incoming students.

Twenty-seven (54 per cent) indicated they had learned to read before entering first grade. It should be noted that another nine (18 per cent) could not remember whether or not they were preschool readers.

Eighteen of the preschool readers stated that they were *taught to read by someone in their family*. Only three of these fifty highly competent readers mentioned a teacher as their source of interest in reading. It is not surprising that the author concludes that educators should give greater recognition to the importance of the child's family in early reading development. Also, as already noted, the data indicate that, among these superior readers, preschool exposure to reading played a more important role than the school in fostering strong interest in reading.

Nor are the findings of Kasdon isolated, for, in fact, studies of highly successful or gifted people show that a high percentage of them had early reading experience. According to Terman's study of gifted children, nearly 50 per cent learned to read before they went to school.[7] Other investigations have produced similar findings. Clear evidence exists that early reading and academic performance are closely related. Many children who have very superior IQ's have difficulty learning to read in the normal school situation and, despite their high level of intelligence, never master reading.

The existence of high IQ "reading problems" in our schools and reading clinics is one of the most serious indictments that could be brought against our present methods of reading instruction. For, functionally speaking, language facility and intelligence are closely related. Language, whether written or spoken, constitutes man's biological advantage over his competitors and if any significant proportion of our intelligent children can not learn to read, it can only be that our methods of reading education are in some way deficient.

The role of environmental stimulation in the realization of intellectual powers has recently been given a great deal of attention. Several leading psychologists have suggested that genetic factors alone are not enough to account for superior performance, and that the environmental influences must be taken into account. As Jerome Bruner has commented, ". . . the intellectual development of the child is no clockwork sequence of events; it also responds to influences from the environment."[8]

The early environment to which the child is exposed plays a crucial role in his intellectual development.

In discussing early readers, for example, William Fowler of Yale wrote:

> Many of these children are ordinarily classified as gifted, but where records are adequate all precocious readers received a great deal of prior stimulation. Consequently, to label a child as gifted in no way dispenses with the necessity of stimulation—if he is to learn.[9]

There is much data which suggests that gifted children are not just of superior native intelligence but have also been provided with proper environmental stimulation. Children of whatever IQ who are denied adequate exposure to learning experiences will never realize their full potential, while children of only average intelligence may be stimulated to surprisingly high levels of performance by environmental circumstance.[10]

Of course, gifted children have inherent aptitudes which explain in part their achievements, but when we realize that in addition to their native gifts, these superior students have had early stimulation from environmental factors, the question naturally arises as to how many other children with high intelligence who never realize their intellectual potential might have become gifted if they had been given more adequate early environmental stimulation. Why is the high IQ student in the remedial reading clinic not fulfilling his intellectual potential? Certainly it is not because of any genetic deficiency in intellectual endowment. And, if he does not have a crippling psychological problem, then to what do we attribute his failure?

We have today growing indications that it is society's failure to understand the nature of intellectual development in the child which is largely responsible for these problems. By not grasping the true nature of the child's language aptitude we are denying many bright children exposure to language at the very time when their brains are best able to absorb this skill. By delaying the teaching of reading until age six and then teaching it under inadequate conditions, we are in effect, condemning a substantial portion of the human race to relative illiteracy.

The remedy for these educational defects in our society is largely in the hands of parents, for only they have control and authority over the child during his most sensitive period of educational development. By exposing the young child to reading, parents will accelerate his language development, reduce the likelihood of his becoming a reading problem, raise to some extent his performance level on intelligence tests, and perhaps even help in the creation of a superior intellect of the highest order.

SUMMARY

Evidence favoring early reading can be found in a variety of completed and ongoing studies and reports. Over the years, a few investigators who were willing to question the dominant doctrine of "reading readiness" have achieved remarkable results in teaching preschoolers to read. These investigators have worked successfully with preschoolers of varying age and IQ.

Recently, there has been something of an "explosion of interest" in the subject of early reading, and a number of studies of varying magnitude and duration have been undertaken which promise to provide additional information concerning how and when reading can most effectively be taught to the preschooler. Television viewing is resulting in the learning of some visual language by large numbers of young children, and TV will likely play an important didactic role in early reading.

The printed format of books (relatively small type, words close together, etc.) has traditionally limited the preschooler's opportunity for adequate exposure to visual language. As new materials continue to be developed, adequate exposure can be achieved. Television, specialized books, and other media presented in the home will tap the preschooler's capacity for early reading. This capacity is but one aspect of his general sensitivity to language; another, as we have indicated, is his mastery of spoken language.

The child who learns to read before entering school is at a decided advantage in the classroom. He is already experiencing success with the single most important task of his educational career. There is considerable evidence that many preschool readers tend to become the most proficient readers. There is also evidence that delaying the teaching of reading can and does contribute to reading problems.

REFERENCES

1. BRZEINSKI, JOSEPH: Beginning reading in Denver. *The Reading Teacher, 18*:16-21, 1964.
2. OREM, R.C.: Preschool patterning and language learning. *National Catholic Kindergarten Review,* Spring, 1966.
3. PENFIELD, WILDER: The uncommitted cortex. *Atlantic Monthly, 214*: 77, 1964.
4. DEUTSCH, MARTIN: The role of social class in language development and cognition. *American Journal of Orthopsychiatry, 35*:78-88, 1965.
5. WALTER, W. GREY: *The Living Brain.* New York, Norton, p. 157, 1953.
6. KASDON, LAWRENCE: Early reading background of some superior readers among college freshmen. *Journal of Educational Research, 52*:251-253, 1958.
7. TERMAN, L.M.: Genetic studies of genius. Vol. I, *Mental and Physical Traits of a Thousand Gifted Children,* Stanford, Stanford University Press, 1925.
8. BRUNER, JEROME: *The Process of Education.* Cambridge, Mass., Harvard University Press, p. 39, 1960.
9. FOWLER, W.: Cognitive learning in infancy and early childhood. *Psychological Bulletin, 59*:133, 1962.
10. HUNT, J. McV.: *Intelligence and Experience.* New York, Ronald, 1961, pp. 347-363.

SUGGESTED READINGS, BRIEFLY ANNOTATED

1. DENNIS, W.: Causes of retardation among institutional children. *Journal of Genetic Psychology, 96*:47-59, 1960.

This study reveals the significant role of stimulation in human development. In a Teheran orphanage in which little stimulation was given the children, Dennis found that 58 per cent of the children between three and four could not sit alone, and only 15 per cent between three and four could walk alone. Dennis concludes that the retardation could be attributed to the restricted environment.

2. Durkin, D. (Ed.): *Reading and the Kindergarten: An Annotated Bibliography.* Newark, Delaware, International Reading Association, 1964.

A twenty-three-item bibliography "to encourage objective and unbiased consideration of the wisdom of earlier instruction . . . at least for some children," says the Editor.

3. Fowler, W.: Cognitive learning in infancy and early childhood. *Psychological Bulletin,* 59:115-152, 1962.

A rather thorough review of the literature of learning in infancy and early childhood shows how the educator's and psychologist's neglect of certain key issues contributed to our low estimate of the young child's potential for learning. Despite experimental and methodological shortcomings, biases, and assorted problems in the field of early learning, it has been demonstrated that early training may influence a child's performance positively in many areas of learning.

4. Frymier, J.: The effect of class size upon reading achievement in first grade. *The Reading Teacher, 18*:90, 1964.

This study was designed to assess the affect of class size upon first grade reading achievement. The small classes achieved, at the end of the first grade, at a significantly higher level than the larger ones.

5. Penty, R.: *Reading Ability and High School Drop-Outs.* New York, New York Bureau of Publications, Columbia University, 1956.

As could be expected, low reading achievement is a major factor operating in a high percentage of drop-outs.

6. Rambusch, N.: *Learning How to Learn: An American Approach to Montessori.* Baltimore, Helicon Press, 1962.

The interaction of teacher, child, and environment in the Montessori format. Montessori methods, materials, and motivational techniques are discussed. Contains an extensive Montessori bibliography of materials in the English language, 1909-1961.

7. Robinson, H.: Promoting maximal reading growth among able learners. *Proceedings of the Annual Conference on Reading at the University of Chicago.* 16: 1954.

See Chap. 17, Reading: a panel discussion, by Ruth Strang, for a summary of a panel discussion by twelve gifted students, dealing with their reading habits.

8. VAN WIE, E.K., and LAMMERS, D.M.: Are we being fair to our kindergartners? *Elementary School Journal.* April, 1962.

How an individualized kindergarten program can give interested five-year-olds a good start in reading.

APPENDIX A

SO YOU WANT TO TEACH YOUR PRESCHOOLER TO READ SOME WORDS?

> Why shouldn't mothers, who spend all day with their children, teach them to read, to understand money, to think about numbers, to understand the calendar, the clock, time, space?
>
> MEAD, MARGARET: Questions that need asking. *Teachers College Record,* 53:92, 1961.

Listening, talking, reading, and writing are all aspects of a central language process. This language process is more basic than the "subject matter" of such school subjects as history or geography. It is, in fact, a "brain function"— an inevitable product of the interaction of any normal human brain and its language environment. Aural language development (listening) and visual language development (reading) are natural functions of human intelligence and would develop naturally under conditions of adequate exposure.

If we talk to a baby (in any language) long enough, then the baby will begin to talk back with intelligent understanding. The same language function can be developed in the child's brain with visual language. The reason so few children have learned to read as they learned to talk is because of the artificial format of the printed page and the size of most type. Conventional type is too small for many children to read, and the nature of the usual page with the words all crowded together give the child little opportunity to grasp their meaning. Where children are exposed to large letters which clearly refer to some person or thing, as in signs or on television, they normally learn to read those words. In order to teach a child to talk, it is only necessary to say words clearly and with reference to definite objects or actions. If we all whispered to children in a rapid mumble, we would have as many talking problems as we now have reading problems.

All normal children master language with no formal instruction. Few adults, even with several years of professional instruction, ever master a new language. The reason is simple; between birth and about five, the human central nervous system has a special language learning aptitude. After that age, other brain functions begin to operate which inhibit and limit the acquisition of new language forms. It is imperative that all language fundamentals be introduced into the central nervous system during its sensitive or formative period in order that the full realization of the language brain function be realized. The law of human development is true for reading as well as speech.

Over the years, many adults, including parents, have successfully taught even very young children beginning reading. Today, home teaching of reading is becoming almost a commonplace. If you are interested in teaching your youngster or youngsters a basic stock of words as a first step to reading mastery, you should find the following annotated bibliography helpful. Most of these references bear directly on the subject of preschool reading. They have been selected by the authors from several hundred such references which have been collected from various publications spanning nearly seventy years. These references provide useful background for the informal preschool reading programs which is described following the references.

BROWN, M.W.: A study of reading ability in preschool children.
An unpublished master's thesis, Stanford University, 1924.

Using a variety of techniques, Brown taught thirteen children (ranging in chronological age from twenty-two to seventy-three months and of varying levels of intelligence) to recognize words and, in some cases, to read from a primer.

BRZEINSKI, J.: Beginning reading in Denver. *The Reading Teacher, 18*:16-21, 1964.

In this study, preschool children were taught certain beginning reading skills. The amount a child learned was related directly to the amount of time someone practiced the beginning reading activities with him. "Because the present study is of a longitudinal nature, final evaluation must await the end of the research project.

Interim results, however, appear to indicate that (1) parents can help their children begin to read; (2) many boys and girls in a large public school system can be taught beginning reading successfully; and (3) such early reading instruction has a measureable, positive, continuing effect." (p. 21)

COHAN, M.: Two and a half and reading. *Elementary English, 38*: 506ff, 1961.

This child learned to discriminate forty words in a relatively short period of time. Praise was used for reinforcement, and the importance of imitation in the preschooler's learning was demonstrated. After learning some words, she developed interest in knowing the names of letters.

APPENDIX A

DURKIN, D.: Children who learned to read at home. *Elementary School Journal, 52*:14-18, 1961.

A group of children who could read when they entered the first grade had received stimulation from family members. One-third of the group had IQ's ranging from 91 to 110. Durkin speaks of the need for an "exposure curriculum."

DURKIN, D.: An earlier start in reading? *Elementary School Journal, 53*:146-151, 1962.

This is a key study indicating the value of early reading experience at home. Durkin followed fifty preschool readers for three years. All were given help in reading at home. After three years, all showed evidence of having profited academically from this experience. Though only fifty children were involved in the study, its pattern matches other reports. This was not a group of gifted children; many had only average intelligence. Durkin notes: "Two observations can be made concerning these fifteen early readers who had intelligence quotients of 120 or less. First they appear to have profited from their early start. Second, the lower the child's intelligence quotient, the greater seems to be the advantage of starting early."

DURKIN, D.: Children who read before grade I: a second study. *The Elementary School Journal.* 54:143-148, 1963.

In this second longitudinal study of early readers, the reading achievement of the early readers is again encouraging. No school problems with reading when children get their initial help in reading during preschool years were found.

DOMAN, G., STEVENS, G., and OREM, R.: You can teach your baby to read. *Ladies Home Journal,* 1963.

This popular article advocated and outlined a simple "game" of word recognition for parents to introduce their children to reading at home in an informal way. Though it was a popular article, it was based in part on a review of the backgrounds of students who learned to read well and made good academic progress in school.

DEWEY, J.: The primary education fetish. *Forum, 25*:315-328, 1898.

"It is a common saying among intelligent educators that they can go into a schoolroom and select the child who picked up reading at home; they read so much more naturally and intelligently."

DAVIDSON, H.: An experimental study of bright, average and dull children at the four-year mental level. *Genetic Psychological Monographs, 9*:119-289, 1931.

In this study, the most extensive of the early experimental investigations of reading in very young children, 3-, 4- and 5-year-old children ranging in IQ from 73 to 139 learned to recognize from 20 to 269 words out of context after about four months' instruction. In view of her results, the author concludes: ". . . it seems that the great amount of time and energy spent on the teaching of reading in the first grade is unnecessary." (p. 255)

>FOWLER, W.: Teaching a two-year-old to read: an experiment in early childhood learning. *Genetic Psychology Monographs, 66*: 181, 1962.

The early reading literature is reviewed and the opposition to early intellectual stimulation is examined. Fowler feels that there is no clear evidence that early intellectual stimulation is damaging to the child.

>GOLDSTEIN, H.: *Reading and Listening Comprehension at Various Controlled Rates.* New York, Teachers College, Columbia University, 1940.

"Reading is apparently a central or general language process rather than a peripheral activity in view of the very high correlations between reading and listening." (p. 62)

>GOODMAN, Y., and GOODMAN, K.: Spelling ability of a self-taught reader. *Elementary School Journal*, 1963.

This study, showing that spelling can be learned naturally without instruction, highlights the importance of individual differences. Kay, the subject of the study, was reading independently, with no instruction, by the age of five and one-half. Less than a year later, she was reading and comprehending material at a fifth-grade level.

>HILDRETH, G.: Early writing as an aid to reading. *Elementary English, 40*:15-20, 1963.

The author notes that preschool children's interest in writing may be utilized in the teaching of reading. In this context it should be remembered that Maria Montessori used a "writing to reading" process in her didactic material. Moreover Dolores Durkin found, in her studies of early reading, a great interest, as well as opportunity, for children to "draw letters."

>HUEY, E.: *The Psychology and Pedagogy of Reading.* New York, Macmillan, 1908, p. 254.

"One can pick out the children who learned to read at home. They read naturally . . . The child does not want to learn reading as a mechanical tool."

>International Reading Association, R. Stauffer, (Ed.): *The Reading Teacher, 18*: 1964.

The theme of this issue is "Preschool and Beginning Reading." There are a number of articles concerning early reading, basically favorable in tone.

APPENDIX A

ISAACS, J.: Should the gifted child be taught to read? *The Gifted Child Quarterly,* 7: 1963.

This article, with a good bibliography of reports of early reading experience, advocates early reading for the gifted child.

McMANUS, A.: The Denver prereading project conducted by WENH-TV. *The Reading Teacher,* 18:22-26, 1964.

This study shows the positive benefits of using TV to instruct parents who are interested in working on prereading skills with their preschoolers. The usual time span for working with the four-year-old was about fifteen to twenty minutes daily.

"The findings at the conclusion of the research study gave unquestionable assurance that the program was worthwhile for parents in working with children." (p. 22.)

"The gains of the experimental group were markedly superior to the gains of the control group. The parents who followed the television course of instruction and used the study guide activities helped their preschool children considerably with prereading skills." (p. 22)

". . . the usual time span for working with the four-year-old was around fifteen to twenty minutes daily . . ." p. 25

OREM, R.C.: Preschool patterning and language learning. *National Catholic Kindergarten Review,* Spring, 1966.

Interdisciplinary evidence which strongly favors early learning in general and early reading specifically is reviewed.

PINES, M.: How three-year-olds teach themselves to read—and love it. *Harper's Magazine,* 226:58-64, 1963.

A discussion of O.K. Moore's provocative work in early reading, including his use of the "talking typewriter."

PLESSAS, G., and OAKES, R.: Prereading experiences of selected early readers. *The Reading Teacher,* 17:241-245, 1964.

Parent questionnaires revealed that a group of twenty selected children who learned to read before grade one were taught by someone. Their learning to read was definitely not a chance happening.

RADER, W.: How much can and should we teach our children? *Elementary School Journal,* 53:137-142, 1963.

Evidence that even very young children are capable of learning more than was once thought has important implications for the objectives of elementary education.

SHAW, J.: Vision and seeing skills of preschool children. *The Reading Teacher,* 18:33-36, 1964.

"From a purely physical point of view, since most normal children can focus and accommodate at the age of twelve months, children's eyes are efficient enough for them to be taught to read at twelve months of age." (p. 35)

"If a child has normal eyes, is in good health and has good intelligence, he can read at an early age." (p. 35)

> SIMMONS, V.: Why waste our five-year-olds? *Harper's Magazine*, *220*:71ff, 1960.

Five-year-olds *can* read.

> SINGER, HARRY: Substrata-factor evaluation of a precocious reader. *The Reading Teacher*, *19*:288-296, 1965.

Analysis of the reading skills of Martha, "a rapid and powerful reader for her age" (5½). Her parents had obtained a tutor for her when she was three.

> STAATS, A., and STAATS, C.: A comparison of the development of speech and reading behavior with implications for research. *Child Development*, *33*:831-846.

The main point of this article is that learning to read and learning to talk are, as learning tasks, more similar than not. If a child has a mastery of spoken language by the age of six, he should certainly be able to master the parallel "visual signal-symbols" of visual language early. Staats notes that where a child with normal speech responses fails to learn to read, the chances are that the problem is not in his IQ or motivation, or heredity. Sibling rivalry or castration anxiety are marginal variables. Staats feels that poor reading is the result of poor instruction—the one possibility most educators never consider.

> STEVENS, G.: A new look at early reading. *National Catholic Kindergarten Review*, Spring, 1964.

The visual reception of words (reading) is but one expression of the general power to think symbolically. Educators may be missing the most natural schedule of visual language development.

> STEVENS, G., and OREM, R.: A new approach to reading for young children. *Building the Foundations for Creative Learning*. (Proceedings of the 1963 American Montessori Society National Seminar), New York, AMS, 1963, pp. 170-187.

All language fundamentals should be introduced into the central nervous system during its sensitive or formative period. This is true for reading as well as speech.

> TERMAN, L.: An experiment in infant education. *Journal of Applied Psychology*, *2*:219-228, 1918.

Martha was probably one of the world's youngest readers. At twenty-four months of age, she had a reading vocabulary of 200 words. Her case is of interest for several reasons. First, it was carefully studied and her progress tested by educators during her preschool period and afterwards—up until the eighth grade. Second, she was taught by her father who was in every respect an amateur as he had no background in either education or psychology, and by his own statement had read no books on the subject of early development or reading instruction. Third, this case is of interest because the father kept records of his techniques and under the sponsorship of Lewis M. Terman of Stanford University, published a detailed case history of his daughter's education.

Terman followed this girl's academic and medical history in grammar school. He reports on her later school adjustment and achievement in his *Genetic Studies of Genius*. According to Terman, she became a superior reader who read rapidly with excellent comprehension. Her IQ tested on several occasions stayed within a few points of 140. Her school record was excellent in every subject with the exception of music and she skipped several grades. Her medical history was normal and all reports indicated that she was normal psychologically and had made a successful adjustment to school and life. By the eighth grade, her ambition was to become a writer and she had already written several little books.

The method by which she was instructed and her response to the instruction illustrates exactly the basic points which the authors of this book have tried to develop. (1) Young children can learn to read and, moreover, enjoy learning to read. (2) The process of teaching them involves three things: Large-lettered words meaningfully associated with objects repeated at frequent intervals. (3) Parents can, with some effort, teach their children to read. (4) Young children should be taught to read since preschool readers become both accurate and rapid readers. (5) The early stimulus of reading may be a factor in the development of a gifted child.

APPENDIX B
A PRESCHOOL READING PROGRAM

OBJECTIVES

To prepare children intellectually for reading by helping them develop a sight recognition vocabulary of from fifty to two hundred words.

To prepare children psychologically for formal reading instruction in the school situation by an informal exposure to reading, in small stages at home.

GOALS OF THE PROGRAM

There is some evidence to suggest that every normal child could become an independent reader before the age of five. But this is not the primary goal of our program. In our opinion, most parents do not have the time to devote to a complete reading program. Most children require some training in phonics to become independent readers, and instruction in phonics is *usually* better left to professional teachers. Our program aims at a sight vocabulary of basic words which will serve as the basis of more advanced reading skills. On the other hand, many children with a little encouragement and informal instruction have become independent readers before school age. There is no reason why once started with our program a child cannot go far beyond its rather modest goals.

WHEN TO START

Believe it or not, there have been examples of simple word recognition in babies under one year, but for all practical purposes, children over two years are easiest to work with. In any event, the essential criterion should be the child's response to the program. No two children have the same pattern of development and some may start early and some late. The child should *never be forced* into the program. If the child does not respond to a relaxed exposure to Part I of the program, wait a month or two and try again. To prepare the child for reading, spend a few minutes at least several days a week reading stories to the child.

THE ONLY DANGER

There is really only one danger in this program and that is completely under the control of the parent. Very young children can learn complex activities, but they do not learn well *under pressure*. The home reading lessons must always be a game, never a chore for the child. Children are very impressionable and can easily be turned against an activity. So long as the child is interested in the "word game," you may continue. But the instant he shows signs of fatigue, *stop the lesson*. Remember you have no schedule to meet. If your child learned one word per week for three years, he would be well on the way to becoming a superior reader.

PART 1

Equipment: One red magic marker and a pack of white cards about 5" by 8". (Note: the heavier the paper, the better.)

Using the style of print on this page, print the child's first name on a card. Make the letters rather thick and about two or three inches high. Make the first letter of the name upper case and the rest lower. Do not be concerned about the names of the letters or the difference between upper and lower case yet.

Then show the card to the child and say in a loud enthusiastic tone of voice, "Johnny" or whatever it may be. Point to the name printed on the card and repeat it several times. You should show a great deal of enthusiasm so that the child senses that these strange red marks have great value. Printed words are initially neutral, unlike pictures or objects, and the child must learn to see their value. Children "catch" an interest from adults. You cannot "tell" a child that something is important; you must communicate it by your tone of voice. After you have repeated the name a number of times, give it to the child, and tell him it is his name. Make up some other copies.

Repeat this whole performance two or three times the first day. If you have a visitor, show them the name and make it an object of some interest. If at any point the child looks at the card or points at it and says his name, then show your approval. Clap your hands; march around the room. This is a major accomplishment! He is on the way! If a child can learn to read one word, he can learn a thousand. That night, tape the child's name over his bed, with much ceremony and allowing him to assist. Every night and morning you can call attention to it. Do the same in the kitchen, and at meal times you can point to it. Within a day or two of these very short periods (no more than two minutes at this point), he should know the word.

When he knows his name go on to "Mommy" or "Mother" whichever you use. Repeat the general procedure, keeping his name over his bed. Now put "Mommy" up in the kitchen. Review his name at bedtime, briefly.

Then go on to "Dad" and the other names in the family. Use the form of the name that is spoken in the family. When the child knows several names, you can begin a guessing game. Let the child match the card with the person. But always keep these activities short and pleasant. *Important Note*: At no point should the child be asked to keep still or quiet or to pay attention. Children learn best when they move about and are free to express themselves. This is a basic rule: Movement and sound are a necessary part of the child's intellectual development!

PART 2

PARTS OF THE BODY

LIST OF WORDS

head	teeth
eye	hand
ear	finger
mouth	thumb
tongue	hair
nose	foot

DIRECTIONS

Print one of the words above on a card. Then show the word to the child and say the part of the body that it names. Do this several times until the child seems to recognize the word.

Then make a game of showing the card and having the child identify it. If he hesitates and does not remember, point to the part of the body named on the card.

As soon as one word is learned, go on to another. Play the guessing game with several words at a time. When the child appears uncertain, give him a clue by pointing to the part of the body named.

If these words are learned in a week and the child's interest in body words seems to be high, then more words naming other parts of the body could be added as the parents elect. In any event, after two or three weeks go on to Part 3 of the program.

PART 3
NAMING THINGS IN THE CHILD'S ENVIRONMENT
LIST OF WORDS

door	table
wall	floor
window	chest (bureau)
bed	closet
picture	book
chair	light

DIRECTIONS

Starting with the word "bed," attach it to the child's bed with some ostentation and with the child's help. Then for a day or two, call the child's attention to the card and have him say the word. When this word is learned, leave it attached to the bed and go on to some other word on the list. Attach each card to the object it names and allow the child to assist in each operation.

When most of the list appears to be mastered, make a game of taking the words down and asking the child to put them back in the correct place. Reinforce his correct response by "overt" enthusiasm. Even if you are by nature somewhat reticent, struggle to overcome your reserve and assume an extroversion for the sake of your child. Your approval manifested in tone and gesture is a key element in establishing motivational sets in your children.

If there are other objects in your home which are of interest to your child, add them to the list. After two or three weeks, move on to Part 4 of the program.

PART 4
ANIMAL WORDS
LIST OF WORDS

dog	lion
cat	bird
mouse	horse
duck	pig
lamb	chicken
cow	elephant

DIRECTIONS

Introduce the animal names one at a time following the same general procedure which has been used in the previous lessons.

When the child knows the list of names fairly well, make a game of matching the sound which the animal makes with his name. Example: the cat says "meow" and cow "moo," etc.

At some point, you can make a game of showing the animal name and asking the child to make the proper sound.

Animal names can be added in accordance with the individual child's interest and experience. Let the child match animal names with pictures of animals cut from magazines and mounted on cardboard squares.

PART 5
COLORS

LIST OF WORDS

red	brown	purple
blue	green	black
yellow	orange	white

DIRECTIONS

Print each word on a separate card. When all the colors are mastered, then try combinations with words already learned. For example: yellow hair, black cat, brown dog, etc. Let the child match cards with colors in his environment—the "brown" card with brown shoes, etc.

PART 6
NUMBERS

LIST: one, two through ten.

DIRECTIONS: SAME AS FOR PART 5. Let the child match cards with quantities of objects—the "two" card with two spoons, etc.

PART 7

LIST OF PHRASES AND SENTENCES

Mommy and Daddy (or Mother and Father)
Mommy and "child's name"
Daddy and "child's name"
Mommy loves "child's name"
Mommy and Daddy love "child's name" etc.

DIRECTIONS

Print one phrase on each card and teach the child in the same informal way used throughout the program. By changing the word order and introducing other members of the family, many other cards can be taught.

PART 8
VERBS AND ADJECTIVES

LIST OF WORDS

Verbs	*Adjectives*
run	big
eat	small
sleep	fast
jump	slow
play	happy
fly	funny

DIRECTIONS

Improvise word games for added fun. For example, have the child act out verbs.

Let the child form combinations of adjectives with nouns he has learned—big dog, happy mommy, etc.

PART 9

At this point, the child has a good background of sight words and the alphabet can be introduced. Alphabet cards can be made up or, even better, one of the many alphabet books available commercially could be used.

INDEX

Absorbent mind, 82
Absorbent Mind, The, 8
Accent, language, 2, 62-63
Advertising, 40
Allport, G., 20
Anderson, I., 26
Andersson, T., 44
Architect as World Planner, The, 2
Artists, xxiii
Association, in language learning, 18
Auto-education, 85
Autonomy, x

Baer, C., 93
Barbe, W., 96
Betts, E., 49
Bible, xxxi
Blocking, perceptual, 53
Bloom, B., xxxiii, xlii, vii, x
Bond, G., 93
Braille, 31
Brain, as computer, 11, 62
Broadcast Education, xix
Brooks, N., 9
Brown, M., xlii, 39
Bruner, J., xli, xiv, 44, 114
Building the Foundations for Creative Learning, xxxv

Canada's World's Fair, xix
Case for Early Reading, The, xxxvii, xvi, xxvii
Cassirer, E., 8
Central Nervous System and Behavior, The, 17
Chicago, University of, xxvi
Child
  as trim tab, xxxviii
  as "worker," 82
Childhood mentality, 8
Class size, 100
Coleman, J., 55
Coming of Age in Samoa, xiv
Comprehensivity, xv
Computers, xiv, xv, xvii
Conant, J., xxxvii, 49, 51

Concentration, child's, xx, 81
Congenitally blind, 61, 62
Conrad, J., 21, 22
Cornell, Dept. of Nuclear Physics, xxiv
Council for Basic Education, 50
Craft tools, xxi
Creativity, xxxvii
Critical period for language, 18
Cumulative deficit phenomenon, 19
Curriculum of Change, xiv

Davidson, H., xlii
Davis, A., 4
Dearborn, W., 26
Defects, in language, 83
Dennis, W., xlii, 17
Denver project, xvii
Deprived, disadvantaged children, 8, 19
Design science
  explorations, xix
  reformations, xxv
Deutsch, M., xlii, 19
Dingman, H., 56
"Direct method," of language learning, 10
Documentaries, xix
Dolch, E., 64
Doll, E., 93
Doman, G., xlii
Doty, R., 17
Durkin, D., xli, 45, 96, 97, 98, 102
Durrell, D., xlii, 56, 71
Dymaxion House, xxix
  map, xvii

Economics, xxviii
Education, as world industry, xviii
Education Automation, xviii
Eidetic imagery, 20-21
Einstein, A., xx
Eisenhower, President, xxv
Emerson, R., xx
Entropy, xxxi
Environmental reading problems, 51
Erickson, E., x
Explosion into language, 81

EXPO '67, xxix
Exposure to language, 16

Father of the Man, 4
Fay, T., xlii
Feral children, 7
Fluid geography, xvii
Ford, H., xxx
Ford Motor Company, xxx
Formative years, 20, 22
Foundling children, 17
Fowler, W., xli, 39, 114
Freedom, 81
Fries, C., xlii, 30, 71
Fuller, R. B., vii, xxx, 2
Functional reading problems, 51, 52
Functions of language, 5

Gates, A., xli, 27, 30, 49, 56, 92, 94
General semantics, 7
Genetic Studies of Genius, 125
Genius, xxx
Geodesic dome, xxix
  Skybreak Bubble, xxix
Geoscope, xv
Gitter, L., xli
Goldfarb, W., 17
Goldstein, K., 16
Gray, W., 49, 50, 69
Greenman, M., 70

Harlow, H., xlii
Harpers, 51
Harris, A., xxxvi
Harrison, M., 91
Havighurst, R., 4
Hebb, D., xlii
Heinze, S., 45
Hermann, K., 27
Heterogeneity, pupil, 100
Home as school, xx
Horne, Dr., xxx
Houses of Childhood, 79
"How to Make the World Work," xxvii
Human Use of Human Beings, The, 18
Hunt, J., xxxiii, xli
Huxley, J., 10

Ideas and Integrities, xii
Imitation, in language learning, 20, 23
Impressionableness of child, 19, 22
Imprinting, 17, 19, 21
Industrialization, xxi
Industrial tools, xxi

Influence of environment, 2
Initiative, x
Intelligence and Experience, viii, 45, 61
Intelligence Quotient, 51, 91, 95-98, 113
"Intensity" of sensation, 29
International Union of Architects,
  Eighth World Congress, xxvi
Interruptions, 102
Inventory memory, 20, 23

Johnson, President, L., xxvi
Joyce, J., 20

Kasdon, L., xlii, 113
Keller, H., 30
Kennedy, President, J., xxvi
Kepes, G., xxiv
King, I., 93
Kopel, D., 95
Korzybski, Count Alfred, 7
Kottmeyer, W., 101

Ladies Home Journal, 49
Langer, S., 8
Langfeld, H., 29
Language and Language Learning, 9
Language as code, 33
  readiness, 75
Learning How to Learn, 39
Left-hand science, xxiv
Life, xvii, 100
Livingry systems, xxv
Lorenz, K., xlii
Lorge, I., 17
Lumsdaine, A., 87
Luria, A., 17

McCarthy, D., 3, 5, 16, 20
McCracken, G., xxxvi, xxxvii, xlii
McHale, J., xviii
MacPhee, H., 45
Man, as "time binder," 7
Manual for Remedial Reading, 64
Marks, R., xvii
Martin, J., xxxiii
Massachusetts Institute of Technology,
  xxiv
Maturation, 61
Mead, M., xiv
Meaning of Meaning, The, 6
Meek, L., 56
Mental Age, 91
Mental form of childhood, 82
Misreading, 53

INDEX

Montessori, M., xli, xxi, 8, 38, 43, 63, 79, 80, 81, 82, 83, 84, 85
Montessori method, xxi
Moore, O., xli, ix, 40
Morgenstern, F., 45
Morphett, M., 91, 92, 94
Morris, D., xi-xii
Morrison, P., xxiv
Music Educators National Conference, xxii

Najarian, P., 17
Natural Education, 39
NEA Journal, xvi
New Yorker "Profile," xxiii
New York Herald Tribune, xxx
Nine Chains to the Moon, xviii
Ninth World U.I.A. Congress, Prague, xxvi

Ogden, C., 6
"One pupil schools," xix-xx
Orem, R., xxxv, xvi
"Organismic" approach to learning, 16
Organization of work, 81
Orton, S., 52

Parents' speech, xxii
Penfield, W., xli, vi, 6, 10
Perrin, D., 87
Physical reading problems, 50-51
Piaget, J., xlii, 8, 45
Pincus, M., 45
Plasticity, of nervous system, 23
Platt, J., xxvi
Poet, xxxii
Portrait of the Artist as a Young Man, 20
Pre-kindergarten child, xvi
Prepared environment, 81
President's Science Advisory Committee, xv
"Prime Movers and Prime Metals," xxvi
Programmed materials, xviii
Psychological reading problems, 51
Psychology of Teaching Reading, 26

"Quality" of sensation, 29
Queen Mary, The, xxi

Rambusch, N., xli, 39
Reading Disability: A Medical Study of Word-blindness and Related Handicaps, 27

Reading failure, first grade, 49
  problems, percentage, 49-50
  readiness, xvi, 71, 75
Reform of environment, x
Reinforcement, repetition in learning, 17
Reversals, 53
Richards, I., 6
Riesen, A., xlii
Right-hand science, xxiv
Right to Learn, The, xxxvi, xxxvii
Roberts, L., vii
Robinson, H., 96

St. Peter's, Rome, xxx
Sapir, E., 16
Saturday Review, x, xix
Science, xxviii
Scientific American, xxvi
Scott, J., xlii
Sensitive periods, 80
Sight recognition- phonics controversy, 69-70
Similarity of reading and hearing words, 27
Sixth Congress of the International Union of Architects, 2
Skinner, B., xli, 36, 89
Sky-Ocean World Map, xvii
Southern Illinois University, xi, xix, xxvii
Speech, 6
  silent, 73
Speech and Brain Mechanisms, vii, 6
Staats, A. and C., xlii, 36, 99
Stability and Change in Human Characteristics, vii
Stein, M., 45
Stevens, G., xxxv, xvi
Stoner, W., xlii, 39
Strang, R., 93
Strephosymbolia, 52
Subvocalization, 53
Synergetics, xiii
Synesthesia, 29
Synopsia, 29

Talking typewriter, ix
Taylor, C., 46
Teacher training, 101
  turnover, 100
Teaching machines, 36
Technology, xxviii
Terman, L., xlii, 39, 125
"Third Parent"—TV, xxvii
Thompson, F., xix

Tinker, M., 93
Touch, x
Trust, x
Two-way TV, xviii, xix
Typography, 37

Uncertified teachers, 100
United States
  Naval Academy, xxxi
  Pavilion, at EXPO '67, xxix

Visual anomalies, 27
von Senden, M., 62, 65
Vygotsky, L., xli, 46

Walter, W., xi, 29

Washburne, C., 91, 92, 94
Washington Post, xv
"Well-documented Case for Teaching Reading Early, The," xxxiii
Whitehead, A.N., 4
"Whole to the particular," xii
Wiener, N., 18, 22
Wiesner, J., xxvi
Witty, P., 46, 95
Wolff, W., 46
Woods Hole Conference, 1959, xiv
"World Literacy Regarding World Problems," xxvi
World
  Resources Inventory, xviii
  Students Design Decade, xxvi
Wright, F., xix